ORDINARY SUPERPOWERS

Unleash the full potential
of your most natural talents

MARK HENSON

DEDICATED TO EVE, WHOSE SUPERPOWERS
MAKE HER THE WORLD'S BEST WIFE,
MOTHER, FRIEND, AND SO MUCH MORE.

ORDERING INFORMATION:

Bulk purchases:
mark@markhenson.me
614-778-8396

Individual sales:
www.amazon.com
www.markhenson.me

ISBN: 978-0-692-85673-4

Library of Congress Control Number:
2017904837

Published in the United States by
The Superpowered Life Company Ltd.

First Edition

TABLE OF CONTENTS

INTRODUCTION

If you're holding this book in your hands, I'm going to guess that you're feeling a wide range of feelings and emotions — curiosity, excitement, a sense of exploration and adventure, and maybe even the tiniest bit of apprehension.

I want you to know that's completely natural.

These are common feelings when you venture a step or two into the unknown, especially when you embark on a journey of self-discovery and improvement. You never know quite what you'll find, do you? You have high hopes that what you're about to experience will fix a lingering problem or help you advance your life in some way. Maybe you're hoping it will clarify your thinking. At the very least, you hope it's mildly entertaining.

This book is all that and more, in my humble opinion. Then again, as the creator of this content, I'd better believe that or I should stop typing right now, huh?

WHO NEEDS THIS BOOK?

People who pick up this book usually feel stuck. Actually, *stuck* isn't the right word. Maybe the word I'm looking for is *lost*. No, *lost* doesn't quite nail it either. *Limbo.* Yeah, *limbo* works. You know, that feeling of being stuck in a holding pattern. You're in motion, but not really getting anywhere.

In limbo, you might actually be doing quite well in your life — good job, happy family, house in the suburbs — but you're not quite firing on all cylinders. Something feels missing; you don't feel fully plugged in. Life is okay, but it's not FANTASTIC. You know there's more you *could* be, maybe even *should* be, doing. You just don't know what that is. So you're stuck. Lost. In limbo. I guess those words do mean the same thing, after all.

On one end of the limbo spectrum, you might even feel as though you're absolutely in the wrong place and doing the wrong things with your time, energy, and resources. You KNOW it ain't right, and you either don't know what to do because you're in limbo, or you're in limbo because you don't know what to do.

Either way, you don't feel as though you're bringing anything special to the world, but you want to. You'd like to feel that you're doing something truly significant or meaningful, but you don't. You're definitely not spending much time, if any, doing the things that light you up, and you DEFINITELY want to.

YOU DON'T HAVE TO CHANGE *THE* WORLD. YOU JUST HAVE TO CHANGE *YOUR* WORLD.

Taken to the extreme, you might even be worried that the clock is ticking, and if you spend another 5, 10, or 20 years in limbo not doing what truly engages and fulfills you, you will have wasted a big part of your life.

Dang, that's heavy. I wasn't planning to go there, but the more I thought about it (and the more I thought about the people I've met through this work), there is some real truth there. I believe we all want to live our lives as fully as possible. I'd like to give you a fighting chance to do that.

WHY YOU SHOULD READ THIS BOOK

I believe to live as fully as possible, to achieve a sense of purpose or meaning, and to truly make a positive dent in the universe (no matter how big or small), there are just three things you have to do:

1. Be 100% you.
2. Love who you are.
3. Make a difference.

Becoming 100% you is a lifelong process for most of us. It involves plenty of trial and error, experimentation and self-discovery, and a willingness to figure out what "100% you" means for you.

Loving who you are is more than just accepting the 100% you that you discover. After all, you can accept something and still not like it very much (like kale salad, for example). But when you truly love something, you can't wait to immerse yourself in it, use it, and share it as much as possible.

Making a difference is what makes our time here on earth worthwhile. It's what we, and others, remember. It's what lasts, sometimes long after we're gone. *Making a difference* can take an unlimited number of shapes and sizes because everyone makes a difference in their own way. Some differences we make are physical — building a hospital wing or a treehouse. Others are emotional — comforting the dying or cheering on a child. Still others are more spiritually focused, such as performing mission work or sharing your faith with someone who wants to understand it.

One thing I want you to understand clearly is this: the size of the difference doesn't matter. I know it sounds aspirational and romantic to "change the world," but I believe with all my heart that you don't have to change THE world. You just have to change YOUR world. And EVERY positive change counts, regardless of size. When I finally realized and accepted that for myself, it took a tremendous weight off my shoulders (and my ego). I hope it does the same for you.

WHAT YOU WILL GAIN FROM THIS MATERIAL

This book offers a path to becoming 100% you, loving who you are, and making a positive difference. It is a simple, yet powerful process that will break you out of limbo and guide you toward a more fun and fulfilling life.

But what is a fun and fulfilling life? There are as many different answers to this question as there are people walking the planet. Your dream could be to build and run a profitable business. Maybe you want to be a healthy and fit role model for others. Perhaps you wish you could improve your community by serving on the city council or the PTA. Or maybe — if you could — you'd simply spend a significant portion of each day creating your art (whatever your art may be).

One of the most direct ways I know to create a more fun and fulfilling life is to *discover what you love doing* that allows you to *contribute at your highest levels* and *help people the most* (or *help the most people* — either way works for me), and then do that as much as possible.

Here's my question to you: *Is that what your life looks like right now?*

For many, the answer to that question is "no." At best, they're doing what they love, contributing at their highest levels, and helping others a *tiny fraction* of each day or week. My goal with this book is to help you transform your focus so you can spend a *significant* amount of your time using your Ordinary Superpowers to make a difference in your life and the lives of those around you. That definitely applies to how you make your living, but it's certainly not limited to your job or career. I know this practice can transform the hours you spend outside of work as well.

Keep reading this book, and I promise you'll discover what your Ordinary Superpowers are. And you'll learn how to use them to create a more enjoyable and fulfilling life.

I'll also share how to activate, enhance, and multiply your Ordinary Superpowers so you can take your powers as far as you wish. You'll learn how and where you can apply your Ordinary Superpowers in places you may not have thought of, how to maximize their effect, and even how to exponentially increase the difference you make by expanding your mission and combining your powers with the powers of others.

WHY LISTEN TO ME?

First of all, while you might be reading my words and following my suggestions, I am only the guide. The person I most want you to listen to is not me, but somebody who knows you way better than I do. That person is you. You're the hero of this story, and this is your journey to take.

I've been on this journey myself for many years. So far, I've had four major careers. I was a radio DJ through college and for several years afterward. I then joined a branding and design consultancy as a copywriter where I spent almost a decade before launching sparkspace, a retreat center for professional and personal development. As I write this, sparkspace is 17 years old. Along the way, I've also become an author, public speaker, and retreat leader. I have an extensive background in creativity work, customer service, and helping teams and individuals bring their best to work and life.

More than 20 years ago, I read *Awaken the Giant Within* by Tony Robbins. That was the first self-help book I ever read. I have read many more since then, and have also experienced countless webinars, retreats, workshops, and seminars. I've taken almost every assessment you've ever heard of (think DISC, Myers Briggs, etc.). I have participated in mastermind groups, hired personal coaches, and participated in "vision days" led by some of the best facilitators in the world. I'm no Tony Robbins, but I have lived and breathed personal development for myself, and with others, for over two decades.

In spite of all this personal and professional development, I found myself experiencing the kind of limbo I mentioned earlier. I was running a great company, making a decent living, and happily married with two kids and two golden retrievers. Yet I wasn't terribly passionate about what I was doing — I didn't feel like I was contributing or making much of a difference at all. Worse yet, I was comparing myself to all the fresh-faced entrepreneurs who seemed to be setting the world on fire — the way I *used* to. I had lost some of my spark, and I found myself missing the old me.

During my limbo, I felt pretty adrift, which is a feeling I simply can't tolerate for long. Although I'm a creative, free-spirit kind of guy, I like to have direction and focus. Whenever I feel adrift, there comes a point when I can't stand it anymore, so I pick a direction and start paddling. This time, the direction I picked was to explore my strengths and passions. I looked at how I was spending my time and how much of it was spent using my strengths. I also looked closely at my strengths to determine which ones lit me up the most and which ones seemed to have the most positive impact on both my mental state as well as the results I achieved for myself and others.

As I used my most powerful strengths more and more, I realized that when I used those strengths, I not only had the greatest impact, but I also gained the most personal satisfaction from using them. I realized too that my most powerful strengths aren't limited to just one part of my life; I use them in many areas. But perhaps the most important lesson I learned was that I was rarely using my most powerful strengths *intentionally*.

When I began to dedicate more and more time to the activities that allow me to contribute my best to my company and help the most people in the process, I started getting some pretty amazing results. Here are just a few:

- I spend 5 times more time doing work that lights me up now. For me, that is creating new initiatives in my business, coaching others, and writing.

- I am no longer captive to my calendar. I have learned how to say "yes" to opportunities where I truly make a difference and "no" to almost everything else.

- I have renewed creativity, which has resulted in fresh ideas for my workshops, my blog, and this book. The workshops have helped hundreds so far, and the blog reaches thousands every week. I hope the book will reach even more.

- I've been able to breathe new life, energy, and excitement into a business that is nearly 20 years old after several years of not feeling passionate about it.

- I've developed an even stronger team that focuses on their most powerful strengths as well, leading to an even healthier company and an incredibly smooth-running operation.

- In my personal life, I have dedicated more time to my wife, kids, and parents, and I've learned how to serve each of them more effectively.

Needless to say, it pulled me out of limbo!

I loved what this renewed focus did for me. So of course, I wanted to share the idea with others. Having spent so much time in personal development, I also realized that what I was exploring and experiencing was a different take on discovering and maximizing my strengths. What made it different was the focus on one's most powerful strengths, the ones that truly set them apart from everyone else.

To me, there was no other word for that kind of strength than *superpower*. And, as I explain in this book, I'm not talking about extraordinary or supernatural talents, but the talents and skills you possess that are *so much a part of you* that to you, they just feel ordinary.

When I finally put those two words, *Ordinary Superpowers*, together, it just clicked. That's exactly what I had been experiencing and explaining to others (just not quite as clearly).

There are many great books about working in your strengths. What makes this one different is that it is simple, straightforward, and focused completely on you and your specific superpowers. It doesn't try to label your strengths. It doesn't try to lump them into a category or bucket. There is no multiple-choice assessment that pinpoints your exact superpowers.

This book is a handbook to help *you* discover how *you* can contribute your best, how *you* can serve others (and yourself) more effectively, and how *you* can make a more intentional, positive difference in the world around you.

HOW TO READ AND USE THIS BOOK

I believe you'll get the most out of this book if you start at the beginning and work straight through to the end, stopping along the way to think and maybe do an exercise or two. This is a quick book to read, and I intentionally didn't cram it full of so many thoughts and activities that you won't have time to explore it all.

Look at it as a bit of a "how-to" guide, mixed with some stories and ideas to inspire you along the way. It is divided into four distinct steps to help you take your Ordinary Superpowers as far as you desire to.

Step 1: Discover
You'll identify the talents and skills that allow you to contribute at your highest levels, help the most people, and give you the most fulfillment.

Step 2: Activate
You'll move from using your Ordinary Superpowers reactively to using them proactively, intentionally, and with purpose.

Step 3: Enhance
You'll grow and improve your Ordinary Superpowers as much as possible to maximize their effect.

Step 4: Multiply
You'll exponentially increase what you can achieve with your Ordinary Superpowers by expanding your mission and collaborating with others.

In each section I suggest some activities to help you think, explore, and capture your progress. I have collected these activities in a companion workbook that you can download for free at **www.markhenson.me/superpowerextras**.

I wanted to provide plenty of practical ideas while keeping the book as short as possible. I don't know about you, but the longer a book is, the less likely I am to finish reading it. If you're a decently fast reader, you can probably whip through this book in a single plane ride.

By the time you've finished the book, you'll have a pretty comprehensive roadmap for incorporating your Ordinary Superpowers more and more into both your personal and work life. When you do, you'll no doubt begin to see evidence of your powerful contribution in the people and world around you. You'll also start to enjoy life more and feel a greater sense of fulfillment. As you do, you'll gain even more confidence in yourself and your Ordinary Superpowers. And you'll want to share them with others.

I'LL MAKE YOU A DEAL

I've heard disheartening statistics on book reading. Some of these statistics say a pretty good chunk of people never even crack open the books they buy. But that's not you. You've at least read this far, so I'd like to enter into an agreement with you. You promise to read at least through **Step 1: Discover,** and I promise to make that section alone worth your time and money, even if you blow off the

LEARNING A NEW
DEFINITION OF SUCCESS
IS A TWO-STEP
PROCESS. FIRST, YOU
HAVE TO UNLEARN YOUR
OLD DEFINITION; THEN
YOU MUST REPLACE IT
WITH A NEW ONE.

rest. I'm suckering you in, of course, because I know that if you take that first step, you will want to take the rest.

One More Thing Before We Begin:

IT'S TIME TO REDEFINE SUCCESS

Before we begin to dig in to your Ordinary Superpowers, there is a crucial first step you must take in order to truly get the most out of this work: **You must redefine what success looks like for you.** If you don't, there's a pretty good chance you'll encounter conflict between your Ordinary Superpowers and what you're trying to achieve in your life.

Think of yourself right now as a young Luke Skywalker. In *The Empire Strikes Back*, Luke has begun his hero's journey from farm boy to Jedi warrior. His whole life, he's dreamed of action, adventure, and fighting evil. He's trained himself the best way he knows how by flying his hovercraft and shooting "womp rats" on his uncle's farm. Then he encounters Obi Wan Kenobi, his first real mentor. Unfortunately, old Obi Wan gets sliced in half by Darth Vader before Luke can complete any significant Jedi instruction.

Enter Yoda — 900 years old and about as experienced as you can get. That's 880 years more life and Jedi experience than Luke Skywalker has when they first meet. As Luke struggles to follow Yoda's instruction, Yoda imparts a powerful lesson that Luke needs to learn before he can move forward. Yoda tells Luke, *"You must unlearn what you have learned."*

Do the same thing, you must.

Just for fun, read the previous sentence out loud in a Yoda voice. (HA! I know you already did!)

From the time you were born, you've been programmed to understand what success looks like. You've been taught that your level of success in life is reflected in the material results of your efforts. These results include position, power, recognition, money, perks, promotions, awards, and the ultimate success cliché: the corner office. The bigger your success, the bigger the material rewards.

The school system taught you this definition as you grew up. The grown-up world reinforced it (and continues to reinforce it every day). And you bought into it — or at least you did until now.

Don't feel bad. Everybody buys into it to a certain degree; it's hard not to. After all, it does carry some appeal. Who wouldn't want a big corner office with a fat leather chair and a view? Sure beats a grey cubicle with a squeaky hand-me-down chair and a view of another grey cubicle. Same goes for money, power, and being showered with praise. Most of us would agree that more of these things beats less of these things almost every time.

Yet...

Material success never equals fulfillment, no matter how much we think we want it or look forward to it. If you've ever purchased a new car, house, or smart phone, you know exactly what I mean. You might really love and enjoy your new car or house or phone. But acquiring those things didn't fulfill you, did it? I know it didn't — because it couldn't. Those things are just things. Shiny, new, novel things for sure, but still just things. One of the biggest mistakes we make as humans is pursuing material results, thinking they will help us feel fulfilled.

WHO IS TRULY FULFILLED AND HAPPY?

Who are the people in your life who seem the most fulfilled and happy? Ask any one of them why they are so fulfilled. I'll bet you ten bucks not one of them will say, *"Because I just picked up my new Audi,"* or *"Because I can see the ocean from my office window,"* or *"Because I won an Oscar."* By the way, if you know someone who won an Oscar, you and I run in vastly different circles, my friend.

Learning a new definition of success is a two-step process. First, you have to unlearn your old definition; then you must replace it with a new one. If you've already denounced your old definition, you've taken the first step. But what if you haven't quite convinced yourself that the material version of success isn't real success? What if you're still thinking that what you most want is that corner office with the big windows?

I feel compelled to pause here and say it's okay to want material things. Material things make life more enjoyable. I'm no monk; I have some nice stuff. I like my stuff. In fact, I recently bought a cabin. It's not a tiny, unheated hunting shack, either. It's a pretty nice cabin on a lake that sleeps ten people and has three bathrooms. It was one of the top things on my bucket list, and I love it. I get a lot of enjoyment out of it. We love letting our friends, family, and employees use it, too.

A cabin on a lake would prompt some people to say, "Now THAT'S what success looks like!" I don't see it that way, though. Although we are able to afford the cabin because of the choices we've made (such as living debt-free, making smart money decisions, and working hard in my business), owning the cabin doesn't make me feel more successful or fulfilled.

What does make me feel successful, however, is what I get to *do* every day. I spend time with my family, I run a business I love, and I get to use my Ordinary Superpowers frequently (which I'll share with you shortly). The common thread here is *doing*. I believe success and fulfillment come from how you choose to spend your time and energy, not in what you acquire, achieve, or possess.

Think about the times when you've felt most fulfilled. Was it when you reached a goal (i.e., achieving), won an award, or gained an object (i.e., possessing) — or was it *while you were striving* to reach the goal (i.e., doing)? Most people I talk to agree that the doing is the truly fulfilling part.

Here's a good test: when you look back on an achievement, what fills you with the most pride? What do you tell stories about — the finished result of your achievement, or the *action, activity, and work it took to get there*? When you look at a trophy, no matter how beautiful and shiny it may be, the trophy is never what you're truly proud of, is it? It is a reminder of what you DID. Why do you think most sports trophies feature a tiny athletic figure frozen in the middle of running, shooting a basket, or hurling a bowling ball?

Do I think we should ignore achievements? Absolutely not! Reaching goals, passing milestones, and finishing projects are all worthy of celebration! In fact, we don't celebrate these things enough. We call them successes, but we don't treat them that way. We blow right by them and immediately shift our focus to the next goal, milestone, or project. Part of our journey — part of our *doing* — should be taking time to enjoy and celebrate our achievements. When we integrate celebrations into our journey, they become a healthy *component* of our success, instead of our end-all-be-all definition.

To move forward from this point, you're going to have to unlearn your old-school definition of success. Here's the catch, though: I don't have a new one to give you. *You have to define success for yourself.* What I can do is help you understand your Ordinary Superpowers so you realize what you're capable of. Once you understand that, you'll have a much better idea of what success might look like for you. And by the way, we're all capable of so much more than we think we are. I hope this book helps you realize that, too.

BEFORE YOU BEGIN

Download the companion workbook at
www.markhenson.me/superpowerextras

STEP

1

DISCOVER

"WHATEVER MAKES YOU WEIRD IS PROBABLY YOUR GREATEST ASSET."

Joss Whedon
(Writer/Director/Producer Superhero)

CHAPTER 1

YOU HAVE SUPERPOWERS (YES, YOU DO)

You have superpowers. Don't believe me? Keep reading; you will.

And if you DO believe me, you're the exception, not the rule. You see, most people I've met don't believe there's anything all that special about them. There is, of course. However, most people don't *recognize* what makes them special. They don't realize they are uniquely qualified to help people *in ways only they can.* They haven't awakened to the idea that they are here to contribute something unique and wonderful to the world around them, possibly even to the *entire* world. But before we go there, let's start at the beginning.

The first step toward maximizing your Ordinary Superpowers is to discover what your powers are. I encourage you to at least be open to the idea that you, indeed, are blessed with a set of abilities that are pretty super, even if you don't know what they are just yet. Coming up, we'll also explore the difference between *Ordinary* and *Extraordinary* Superpowers and why you don't need Extraordinary Superpowers to make a positive contribution and experience more fulfillment in your life.

It's not that people don't *want* to see their own superpowers. It's just that they are blind to them. In fact, I believe all of us are *born* blind to our own superpowers. Your most important job while you're here on this planet is to figure out how to be 100% you. One of the most direct and powerful ways to do that is to discover your superpowers. Another is to use those powers as much as possible.

There's a quote that has been attributed to everyone from Mark Twain to Picasso: *"The meaning of life is to find your gift. The purpose of life is to give it away."* No matter who said it, I think it hits the nail on the head.

Remember Jimmy Stewart's character, George Bailey, from the movie *It's a Wonderful Life*? George never understood how his actions had positively impacted everyone around him until it was (almost) too late. Sadly, many people live their entire lives without knowing how they contribute the most to their friends, families, workplaces, and communities. They never know how much they positively affect those around them. They never understand how much more they could do — often with little extra effort — to make a big difference. They never realize just how much more satisfaction, fulfillment, and enjoyment they could generate in their own lives by discovering and using their own superpowers. But that's not going to happen to you, right?

Repeat after me: I will NOT be like George Bailey.

ORDINARY SUPERPOWERS, DEFINED

Ordinary Superpowers are the talents and skills you possess that enable you to contribute at your highest levels, help the most people, and experience the most fulfillment in life.

In other words, they are the talents and skills that enable you to create positive change in your life, the lives of others, and the world around you.

They're called "Ordinary" Superpowers because, as powerful as they may be, there is a high likelihood that they don't feel special to you. They often feel so natural to you that you assume everyone else has them, too. To you, they just feel *ordinary*. However, as you learn more about them, you'll realize they are the "secret sauce" that makes you, well, you. By Discovering, Activating, Enhancing, and Multiplying them, you'll powerfully and positively improve your life and the lives of the lucky people around you.

DOES EVERYBODY HAVE SUPERPOWERS?

Yep, we've all got 'em. Your kids have them. My friends have them. That guy in the next cubicle has them, and the woman you saw standing at the bus stop this morning has them. Plumbers, preachers, and business professionals have them. I'd even argue that newborn babies have them (I defy you to resist smiling when a baby smiles at you).

Our superpowers are how we get stuff done. They are how we solve many of our problems, and how we add the most value to our projects and to the lives of others. Superpowers are truly what makes the world go 'round, and 99% of the time we are not even aware that we are using them. Ninety-nine percent is not a scientifically proven number, by the way; don't get hung up on it. I'm just trying to make a point.

Our superpowers are an integral part of who we are. They're just what we do; they're how we roll every day, whether we're aware of them or not.

For that reason, to us they're just — you guessed it — *ordinary*.

My superpowers don't seem all that super to me. Yours don't seem all that super to you. It's not true, of course. Just ask anyone around you what they think about your Ordinary Superpowers (once you discover what they are) and they'll tell you things like, *"I'd kill to have that ability,"* or *"I wish I had your skill,"* or *"You're nuts if you don't think that's a superpower."*

That's why I wrote this book — to help you discover your Ordinary Superpowers and begin to use them more proactively. Actually, *discover* might be the wrong word. *Uncover* might be a more accurate description for revealing something that's already inside of you, working behind the scenes to make good stuff happen for you and others. I want to help you pull back the curtain so your Ordinary Superpowers can shine, and so you can make an even more powerful, positive impact on the world around you.

YOU WEREN'T GIFTED WITH EXTRAORDINARY SUPERPOWERS — SO WHAT?

I will never win a talent show like *American Idol, The Voice,* or *The X-Factor.* I simply wasn't gifted with a voice that moves people to tears (not in a good way, anyway). Sure, I can carry a tune and I sound pretty good singing along with Frank Sinatra, AC/DC, or Justin Timberlake in my car. But that's as far as it goes.

ORDINARY SUPERPOWERS ARE THE TALENTS AND SKILLS YOU POSSESS THAT ENABLE YOU TO CONTRIBUTE AT YOUR HIGHEST LEVELS, HELP THE MOST PEOPLE, AND EXPERIENCE THE MOST FULFILLMENT IN LIFE.

I will never figure out complex math problems like Matt Damon's character in *Good Will Hunting*. Only so much brainpower in my noggin, and almost all of that is being expended to write this book.

I'll also never win a People's Choice Award for my acting ability, a Nobel Peace Prize for my philanthropic efforts, or an Edward R. Murrow Award for my skills in journalism. Although, on a side note, my incredibly talented wife DID win a national Edward R. Murrow award (our nation's highest award for journalism) while she was a television news reporter. I, of course, can take no credit for that whatsoever.

Oh, yeah, I'll also never fly, shoot webs from my hands, or deflect bullets with my mind like the comic-book and movie superheroes.

Those kinds of talents are NOT Ordinary Superpowers. They are *extraordinary* superpowers, and yes, they are awesome. We hold those kind of superpowers in such high regard because they are truly rare. *The truth is, though, most of us don't have extraordinary superpowers.* I know, I know, that's not what your momma might have told you. But that's a momma's job — to let her kids know how special they are, to give them a hint that they have something great to contribute to the world. A momma's job is to tell her kids they can be anything they want to be and to say, "*Baby, your voice is so beautiful you could win* American Idol." Even when the voice sounds like fingernails on a chalkboard.

Your momma may have been wrong about your ability to hold a tune, but she was right about one thing: you DO have something great to contribute to the world. As you identify your Ordinary Superpowers, you'll find that you're *already* contributing something great to those around you, and you're not even aware that you're doing it. As you Discover, Apply, Enhance, and Multiply your Ordinary Superpowers, I'm pretty sure you'll end up positively impacting the world more than most of those contestants on *The Voice* ever do.

If you think you need a rare skill, talent, or ability to make a difference, stop thinking that way! Stop waiting for an extraordinary superpower to emerge before you decide to proactively contribute on a higher level to your job, family, community, and planet.

Whether you have any truly extraordinary superpowers or not, I *guarantee* you have some Ordinary Superpowers (probably more than you suspect). As you discover more about your own powers, you'll come to know that they, too, are more extraordinary than you think.

By the way, if you DO have an extraordinary superpower, by all means USE IT. Share it. Cultivate it. Let that light shine! Extraordinary superpowers can always find a noble purpose, such as bringing joy to others, inspiring the discouraged, or solving difficult and complex problems — all things the world needs in much larger doses. Imagine what the world would have been like if Albert Einstein, Prince, or Michael Jordan had decided to not share their extraordinary gifts with us.

For the rest of us who missed out on the genetic jackpot, know this: we can do equally amazing and noble things by taking the four steps toward maximizing our *Ordinary* Superpowers.

Even though we're just getting started, you've already made progress. You've started to believe in Ordinary Superpowers, and you've begun to wonder just what yours may be (I know, I can see it in your eyes). You also know that whatever powers you may have do not have to be extraordinary to make a difference. And that's the perfect place for you to be right now.

CHAPTER 2

WHY DO WE LOVE SUPERHEROES (AND SUPERPOWERS) SO MUCH?

We can't talk about superpowers without mentioning a superhero or two, so I thought I'd get it out of the way right now. And while this book isn't about comic book and movie superheroes, they do have some pretty admirable qualities worth talking about, and worth striving for.

To start this little superhero chat, I have a confession to make: as a kid, I played superhero a lot. I'd frequently stay in my superhero fantasy world long after mom rang the dinner bell. Much to my dismay, even superheroes had to stop fighting crime long enough to eat their vegetables.

I played superhero so much, my mother finally made me a cape. She probably got tired of me dirtying up her beach towels. Or maybe she was terrified I would accidentally strangle myself by tying a towel in a knot around my neck and getting caught on a fence somewhere. Whatever the reason, I got a "real" cape out of the deal. It was black, just past butt-length (an acceptable length for any respectable superhero), and had a snap-button collar that my little fingers could easily snap together. It was brilliantly designed so that it would also easily *unsnap* if I got it caught on, say, a fence somewhere.

Although I sometimes would let my imagination transform me into Superman, Spider-Man, Iron Man, Luke Skywalker and others, my default alter ego was always Batman. I liked the fact that he was just a normal, brilliant gazillionaire. He wasn't a mutant, like Spider-Man, or an alien, like Superman; he didn't have an extra dose of the Force, like Luke Skywalker. He was just a regular guy — more or less — that took full advantage of his talents and resources. In truth, my choice may have also been influenced a bit by the fact that Batman had a black cape and an awesome mode of transportation.

I know I'm not alone in my childhood superhero play. Almost everyone I speak to had a superhero phase. You might think it's a boy thing, but it's not. A surprisingly high number of women I speak to also admit to a secret superhero past. Some never outgrow it (only now we play it in our basements, in secret, late at night, on our Xbox). It's no wonder why an increasing number of superheroes have leapt from the pages of comic books and landed on movie-theater screens around the world.

Superheroes have existed as long as man has walked the planet. Even before modern-day Spandex superheroes made their way to the big screen, stories of legends, heroes, demigods, and deities that people turned to for help in times of need were passed on from generation to generation.

What was it about superheroes that drew us to them as kids? Why did we want to BE them so badly when we were younger? When I ask participants at my retreats those questions, the answers I hear include:

"They're strong."

"They're confident."

"They help people."

"They save the day."

"They defeat the bad guys."

"They do things normal people can't do."

"People admire them."

"They're good-looking."

"They always get the hot girl/guy."

All of that felt possible every time I snapped on that cape, ran around the yard, and jumped out of a tree as a kid. And I will freely admit those are all pretty much the same things I still want as an adult, minus the "jumping out of a tree" part.

I want to be strong; I want to be confident; I want to save the day. I'd say I want to get the hot girl, but luckily for me that has already happened. I do want to keep her around for the next 50 or 60 years, though.

It's not necessarily about being rich, famous, or some kind of superhero rockstar. We might chase some of those things when we're young, but over time, most people feel the pull to fulfill their potential and contribute at their highest level, regardless of worldly rewards, accolades, or traditional "success."

I'm guessing you probably want similar things for your life.

Here's a little secret: When you discover your Ordinary Superpowers and you start to use them more proactively, you will start experiencing more superhero-like results. I can't promise you'll get the hot guy or girl, but I can tell you that you'll be several steps closer to becoming 100% you, loving who that is, and using that person to make a positive difference. You'll become more confident, you'll feel stronger, you'll help more people, and you might even save the day once in a while.

OKAY, ENOUGH ABOUT SUPERHEROES. THIS BOOK IS ABOUT YOU.

To be clear, this is NOT a book about superheroes (not the movie kind anyway). It's about the powers you and I possess, not the supernatural abilities of a "chosen one." There's a big difference. I am in no way implying that any of us should aspire to become an action-movie superhero.

This book, this work, this idea, is about *Ordinary Superpowers*, which means it's for ordinary people like you and me. I believe we ordinary folk can achieve extraordinary things, especially when we learn how to maximize our Ordinary Superpowers.

Besides, although we all aspire to achieve superhero-like results, most of us wouldn't look good in those skin-tight superhero costumes anyway. I mean, I'm confident, but I'm not THAT confident. Are you? Capes, however, look good on everybody. If you've got one, go ahead and put it on while I dive into a deeper definition of what an Ordinary Superpower is.

WHEN YOU DISCOVER
YOUR ORDINARY
SUPERPOWERS
AND YOU START TO
USE THEM MORE
PROACTIVELY, YOU WILL
START EXPERIENCING
MORE SUPER-
HERO-LIKE RESULTS.

CHAPTER 3

WHAT, EXACTLY, IS AN ORDINARY SUPERPOWER?

If you're going to Discover, Apply, Enhance, and Multiply this stuff, it might be helpful to know exactly what I'm talking about when I say Ordinary Superpower, huh?

The quick definition is this: Ordinary Superpowers are the talents and skills that enable you to contribute at your highest levels, help the most people, and experience the most fulfillment in life. They are how you create positive change in your life, the lives of others, and the world around you.

The rest of this chapter provides a much more detailed description of what Ordinary Superpowers are. By the end of this chapter, you should be well on your way to identifying what yours may be. I'll also share a simple test to help you separate your Ordinary Superpowers from the rest of your many, many fine (but non-superpower) talents.

To begin with, Ordinary Superpowers exhibit the following characteristics:

THEY ARE REMARKABLE

We all have talents and skills. Some are quite common — walking, talking, and the ability to chew gum. These are things most people do with ease and proficiency. However, you also possess some powers that are *not* common to everyone.

A remarkable ability (or talent or skill) doesn't necessarily mean an extraordinary ability (although it can be). It also doesn't mean it is unique, implying you're the only one in the world who has it. It simply means that *you have noticeably more of it, or you are better at it, than most of the people around you.* For example, you may not be Tony Robbins, but you can still deliver a darn good presentation when you need to. You know there are other great presenters in the world, but among your friends and colleagues, you're definitely considered one of the best.

Most people actually have more than one remarkable talent or skill. That's why I almost always put an "s" on the end of the words *Ordinary Superpowers*. There is a good chance you don't even recognize all of your own Ordinary Superpowers yet. That's okay, you will soon.

THEY FEEL NATURAL TO YOU

When you identify the remarkable talents and skills that you possess (as defined above), you may notice that these are things that you've done for a long time, maybe even your whole life. Even if you've recently developed what you consider to be a unique skill, chances are it came somewhat naturally to you. Sure, some hard work could have been involved, but a unique ability, talent, or skill is most often something you're born with, or at least born with an aptitude for.

Natural ability or aptitude comes with a weird downside, though: there's a tendency to not realize how remarkable and super it really is. We think if it's easy for us, then it must be easy for everyone (and therefore, we don't recognize its true power or value).

This is the one time you're allowed to compare yourself to other people. Size up your powers against the people around you. Do they have the same powers? Probably not. If they do, do they have a larger than average (i.e., remarkable) dose of them like you do? Pretty sure the answer, again, is no.

Can an Ordinary Superpower be something that doesn't come naturally to you, but instead is something you've worked hard to develop? Absolutely, but understand there is a difference between a strength and a superpower. To determine which is which, look at all the characteristics in this chapter before deciding whether something is truly one of your Ordinary Superpowers or just something you're pretty darn good at doing.

YOU USE THEM IN MANY PARTS OF YOUR LIFE

If you had the power of invisibility, you'd use it in just about every part of your life, right? You'd use it when you didn't want to be disturbed at work, or to follow your kids on dates. You'd sneak up on people and scare the bejeezus out of them every chance you could. Okay, that last one is probably something only I would do, not a fine, upstanding person like yourself. (Or would you?)

You most likely use your Ordinary Superpowers at work, home, and most other places you spend time. You use them with friends, family, and strangers alike. Since they come naturally to you, it's only natural that you automatically use them whenever and wherever the need arises.

For example, I have a friend who has the superpower of *bringing together people with similar interests*. It's no surprise that he loves hosting dinner parties for friends and family. And that same superpower makes him a darn good salesperson at work.

I suspect that if you don't use your remarkable powers in more than one part of your life right now, you know in that superpowered brain of yours that you probably *could*.

YOU ENJOY USING THEM

This is where you start to separate your strengths from your Superpowers. For something to qualify as an Ordinary Superpower, it must pass the enjoyment test: when you use one of your remarkable talents or skills, does it *fill* you with energy or *deplete* you of energy? In other words, do you *enjoy* using it?

One of my remarkable talents is fixing technology problems. I'm better at it than most people I know. Because of this, I often end up playing the part of tech support for myself, my company, my wife, my kids, and my parents. Can I troubleshoot and fix most problems? Yes. Do I enjoy it? *Not one bit.* Does it give me energy? Just the opposite. It drains my very soul. I actually *hate* fixing technology problems, even though I've got some mad skills in this area. For that reason, it may be a remarkable skill, but it is definitely NOT one of my Ordinary Superpowers.

On the flip side, I hate anything that is unnecessarily complicated. I am always finding ways to simplify how ideas are communicated, how processes are structured, and even how the cupboards in my kitchen are organized. This isn't just a remarkable skill, however; it's a remarkable skill that I LOVE using. I get so much satisfaction when I simplify just about anything.

THEY GET SUPER RESULTS

Any power that doesn't yield super results can't really be considered a superpower, now can it? This is another good test to distinguish between a unique ability, talent, or skill and an Ordinary Superpower.

You might be able to eat fifty hot dogs in one sitting, but unless you're on the hot-dog-eating contest circuit, it would be hard to identify a result that was anything close to super. However, if you have the unique skill of *organizing a list of tasks into an efficient workflow*, that can lead to pretty super results. And that sounds like an Ordinary Superpower to me.

THE TEST

I'm a big believer in keeping things simple. Most things in life are not rocket science, and we shouldn't try to make them that way. To qualify something as an Ordinary Superpower, you can apply this simple, four-part test:

1. It comes naturally to me.
2. Most people DON'T have this power.
3. It helps people.
4. I enjoy using it.

THE REAL SUPERMAN

Like many young boys, I thought my dad was Superman growing up. Not the tights-and-cape-wearing Superman, but a real *super man* — strong, smart, kind, and helpful.

THE TEST OF AN ORDINARY SUPERPOWER:

1.

IT COMES NATURALLY TO ME.

2.

MOST PEOPLE DON'T HAVE THIS POWER.

3.

IT HELPS PEOPLE.

4.

I ENJOY USING IT.

My dad is a great teacher. Most of his career, he taught in high schools. He was in his element working with high-school kids. I know this because I had him for a teacher and was privileged to witness his ability in this area firsthand. One of my dad's Ordinary Superpowers is to *always see the best in people and the good in any situation.* That should be a common trait among teachers, but you and I both know it is not. If it were, we'd all have more than just one or two teachers who made a big difference in our lives.

Dad was that teacher who would step into the middle of a hallway fight, pull the combatants aside, look them in the eye, and say, *"Why are you two knuckleheads fighting? You're better than that. You're smarter than that."* Yes, he actually used the word *knucklehead.* Most teachers would get reprimanded for calling a student a name like that, but dad liked and respected the kids so much (and vice versa) that he got away with it. He always saw the good, even in the "bad" kids. He always helped them see a way out. He always gave them a chance.

My dad's superpower also showed up in the way he served his church, family, friends, and community. Throughout my life, I witnessed him helping people that nobody else even wanted to be around. There was a particular woman in our church who was as mean and nasty as they come. Yet for years, dad would drive out of his way to pick her up and bring her to church on Sunday mornings because she couldn't drive. He worked hard to see the good in her and always tried to help her see the good in herself. She liked my dad better than anyone. At least I think she did, because she always seemed to be a tiny bit less mean and nasty to him than to everyone else.

As an example, let's see how that Ordinary Superpower of my dad's passes the test:

1. **It comes naturally to him.** *He always tries to see the good in other people. It's his default setting.*

2. **Most people DON'T have this power.** *He has this ability more than most people I have ever known.*

3. **It helps people.** *He uses this power to assist people in need, even when they're not the easiest people to help.*

4. **He enjoys using it.** *When he gets a tough cookie to crack a smile, you can tell it's his favorite thing in the whole world to do.*

My mom also has superpowers. One of hers is *making a home look spectacular*. I grew up in a middle-income family; Dad was a high school teacher, and mom worked in an elementary school principal's office. I, too, spent a lot of time in an elementary school principal's office, but that's a story for another book.

Even though we didn't have tons of money growing up, my mom still made our house look like a million bucks. The house I grew up in was all of about 1500 square feet, but my friends always commented about how nice it was. And when high-school kids notice something like that, you can bet it was pretty noticeable (one might even say *remarkable*).

My mom will be turning 80 the year this book comes out, and the house she and dad currently live in looks like something out of a magazine. They're getting ready to move to a retirement home, and I'm willing to bet they'll have the nicest-looking apartment in the whole complex.

Mom's decorating power definitely passes all four parts of the test. But when I tell her she could be an interior designer, she doesn't necessarily believe me (although it is SO true), which, of course, is quite typical of an Ordinary Superpower.

BORN — OR TRANSFORMED?

Are people born with their Ordinary Superpowers, or are superpowers the result of a transformation later in life (and by later I mean after puberty)?

I'm no genetic scientist, but I think it's safe to assume that if someone has a superior skill before they are 10 or 12 years old, they were likely born with that superpower — or at least the raw materials for it. I know young kids who have the innate ability to make people laugh, or throw a mean curve ball, or even see through someone else's BS. Could you imagine how much stupid stuff you could avoid in life if you always had the ability to sense when someone was full of crap? Ah, but this is not a book about the abilities we WISH we had, so I must move along.

Some people are late bloomers for sure. Their Ordinary Superpowers show up later in life for no apparent reason other than they were in the right place at the right time for their superpowers to emerge. It is possible that sometime in your adulthood, you'll recognize a superior talent that seems brand new to you. You'll have an "Aha!" moment when you think to yourself, *"Huh, I didn't know I was so* compassionate," or *"I was never this organized before,"* or *"WOW, I'm REALLY good at coaching teenage girls recreation league basketball."*

Sometimes these talents have been there all along, and they've just been hiding behind all the other stuff you do every day. You've never had much opportunity to use them, so when the chance arrives, you're taken a little by surprise at how easy and fun using your "new" superpower is. These powers are easier to recognize than the ones you've been using all along, simply because they feel new to you. The novelty makes them stand out.

There is a difference, though, between a fun new skill and a true Ordinary Superpower. To differentiate between the two, apply the test of a superpower:

1. It comes naturally to me.
2. Most people DON'T have this power.
3. It helps people.
4. I enjoy using it.

Since we're talking about newly discovered superpowers right now, I feel the need to add a qualifying question to the fourth step of the test. As humans, most of us are wired to enjoy pleasurable new experiences. There is definitely pleasure to be experienced in using your newfound talents — at first. The qualifier for a true Ordinary Superpower is this: *Do you still enjoy using it AFTER the novelty wears off?*

Just because an Ordinary Superpower mysteriously shows up after you've become a grownup doesn't mean that you weren't born with it. Once you recognize an Ordinary Superpower, you may be able to take a trip down memory lane and see traces of your superpower in many parts of your past.

For instance, maybe you've discovered you have a real knack for seeing potential new uses for old, worn-out, or even broken objects. You recycle castaway items (that someone else considered junk) into affordable, whimsical art that makes people happy.

Looking back, you might have always had that ability; you just never expressed it in such an artistic way. Maybe you kept your grandmother's dishes, not because you wanted to use them for Thanksgiving dinner, but because you liked the way they looked in your china cabinet. Maybe you cut old jeans into jean shorts. Or maybe you always washed and re-used the plastic containers from your favorite take-out restaurants. You might argue that you just hate to throw things away, but I could just as easily argue that one of your Ordinary Superpowers is — and possibly always has been — giving things new life and purpose.

Another example: at your current age, you've been told for the first time you are really good at quickly finding information that adds value to a conversation or helps solve a problem. You've never considered yourself a researcher before, but when you think about it, you remember a time when you cruised by a store just to see the posted shopping hours because your wife will be shopping there later. Or you were curious about something you read in a magazine, so you immediately popped on Amazon.com to search for a book (or ten) on the topic. Of course you bought one (or ten) because you have — and always have had — information curiosity as an Ordinary Superpower. I just made up the name for that power, but you get my point, right?

Now that power is clearly surfacing in your life because of the work that you're doing, or a challenge you've been asked to overcome, or because it is necessary in order to reach a goal. So, it could be a combination of what you were born with and how you've been transforming in your life along the way.

To sum up this section, I feel the need to answer this question once and for all: Do I think you might have been born with your Ordinary Superpowers, or do I believe you could have transformed later in life and developed powers that didn't exist for you before?

My answer is yes.

Now that you have a super in-depth, comprehensive and exhaustive understanding of what an Ordinary Superpower is, and you're equipped with the test to help you positively identify your own, you're as ready as you're ever going to be to dig in and discover what makes YOU so darn powerful. Let's go!

CHAPTER 4

DISCOVER YOUR ORDINARY SUPERPOWERS

You have *hundreds* of abilities, talents, and skills. For each one, you possess a current level of mastery, from novice to expert. Some of them you enjoy, and some you don't. Some you use every day; others lay dormant for long periods of time. You share some in common with almost everyone, and a handful are unique to you.

But which ones are Ordinary Superpowers? It can be hard to tell, especially when something doesn't quickly jump out at you.

I've met some people who have incredibly clear superpowers. They know exactly what they are, and they proactively use them to create powerful and positive results. How did they figure it out? A few of them were just blessed with self-awareness from an early age. But the majority of the people who understand their superpowers did some work to discover them. They may have recognized over time what works extremely well for them, or they may have explored books, workshops, or assessments such as *Strengthsfinder 2.0* by Tom Rath, *StandOut* by Marcus Buckingham, or one of the many other ways to discover strengths, motivation, and more. The book in your hands right now is (hopefully) one of those helpful resources, too.

It's time to start discovering what *your* Ordinary Superpowers are. But how? Well, that's exactly what this chapter is about. You'll start by examining your life's activities and the talents you use frequently (maybe even more than you realize). Then you'll apply the simple test I explained in the previous chapter, along with some additional thinking, to help you narrow your list of potential superpowers down to your top three. I'll also explain why that is imperative.

THE 6 QUESTIONS THAT REVEAL YOUR ORDINARY SUPERPOWERS

There are six questions I've found helpful to begin identifying the abilities, talents, and skills that may be Ordinary Superpowers:

1. What are you always doing?
2. What do people always ask you for help with?
3. What do you always feel compelled to volunteer for?
4. What do you do that other people admire?
5. What do you do that makes a positive difference?
6. What do you enjoy doing the most in the whole world?

Let's look at these questions one by one.

1. What Are You Always Doing?
The first clue to an Ordinary Superpower is to take a look at what you're always doing. There are three things we find ourselves always doing:

1. *We always do what we absolutely have to do.* We have to go to work. We have to feed ourselves and our families. We have to transport ourselves from place to place. We have to take care of emergencies.

2. *We always do what's easy.* C'mon, admit it, we all tend to do the easy stuff. We're humans, it's how we operate. By the way, *easy* doesn't always mean "unimportant." There are many things we consider to be easy that are useful, important, and even necessary. But given the choice between easy and difficult, we will (almost) always choose easy.

3. *We always do what we're wired to do.* When something comes naturally to you, or you're particularly good at something, you tend to do it frequently because it's your default setting; it's what you gravitate to.

An ordinary superpower could fall into any of these categories and certainly could be a combination of two or more, particularly something that is both easy and comes naturally. While those two characteristics are independent of each other, they often go hand-in-hand. Makes sense, doesn't it? If something comes naturally to you, it's likely to seem easy.

Don't ever discount what comes naturally and easily to you. We tend to think that if something is easy for us, it's probably easy for everyone. That's simply not the case. What's easy for you may be mind-boggling for me. What comes naturally to me, you may struggle to develop competency in.

I use this example all the time: numbers, spreadsheets, and Quickbooks reports make my head spin. They're like a foreign language to me, and I struggle to wrap my brain around them. My longtime bookkeeper, Carol, though, can create, analyze, clean up, and completely understand numbers and spreadsheets in her sleep. I wouldn't be surprised if she dreams about them, and enjoys the dreams, too.

On the flip side, I have no fear of standing on a stage and speaking to 10 people or 10,000. When I was 24 years old, I emceed the 4th of July fireworks celebration in Lansing, Michigan in front of 50,000 people. Didn't phase me at all — it's just something I've never really had a fear of. I personally know dozens of people who would have a heart attack and die on the spot if I asked them to read a single sentence into a microphone in front of a crowd. It took me a long time to recognize how unique that talent is, but now I recognize it as one of my superpowers.

When we think it's natural or easy for everyone, we discount the value of that ability, and we don't realize how special, and unique, and powerful that ability may be. We simply think it's ordinary (hence the term "Ordinary Superpower").

2. What do people always ask you for help with?
When you review the types of tasks and activities that people ask you for help with, you'll probably see patterns quickly. You might even find yourself frequently wondering things like:

"Why do people always ask me to help them fix their computer?"

"Why do people always want to talk to me about how to deal with an unhappy toddler?"

"Why do I always get asked to join the committee to plan the company party?"

If you've ever asked yourself one of these kinds of questions, I'm willing to bet you just let it hang there and never really answered it. You may have even asked it out of frustration because someone asked you to do that thing AGAIN. If that's the case, I'd like to challenge you to shift the focus of the question.

When we're frustrated by a request, we ask the question in a whiney, complaining tone. You know what I mean. As an example, read this sentence in your head in THAT voice, emphasizing the capitalized words:

"WHY do people always ask ME to help them fix their computer?"

Now, change the tone of your question. Ask it in the spirit of actually wanting to know the answer instead of using the question to vent your frustration. I'll even rewrite it a little bit to help you shift the tone. Now try it again, using a much more inquisitive and pleasant tone in your head:

"Hmmmm, I wonder...Why DO people always ask ME to help them fix their computer?"

What you're asking with this rephrased question is, "What talents and skills do other people clearly see in me (that maybe I don't even see in myself)?" This is such a great exercise because quite often other people see our uniqueness much more clearly than we do. They see the results our abilities produce, and they make the connection. We, on the other hand, see those things as just what we do, and often overlook them.

3. What do you always feel compelled to volunteer for?

Have you ever been in a charity, community group, or PTA meeting where a particular task or role is being described, and then they ask for someone to volunteer to take on that task or role? I've been there, and there are typically two reasons I feel compelled to actually volunteer:

1. Absolutely nobody else is volunteering for a task that needs to be done. As in — everybody is avoiding eye contact with everybody else, hoping no one directly asks them to take on the task. My sense of obligation, responsibility, or compassion usually prompts me to raise my hand in these situations.

WE TEND TO THINK THAT IF SOMETHING IS EASY FOR US, IT'S PROBABLY EASY FOR EVERYONE. THAT'S SIMPLY NOT THE CASE.

2. The task plays to my strengths. I know I could do it with one hand tied behind my back because it's right up my alley.

Volunteering for the first reason often leads to regret, frustration, and gnashing of teeth. However, when the second reason leads me to volunteer, that might be a nudge from the universe that maybe, just maybe, my Ordinary Superpowers are being called into action. When we know we're good at doing something, we gravitate toward opportunities that will benefit from that strength. We even feel compelled to volunteer for tasks that, on the surface, *might not even appear to be fun*, but we instinctively know we can perform them better than anyone else in the room.

4. What do you do that other people admire?

While some people actively seek out the admiration of others, I've found that most people have a hard time with this one. Unless we have an extraordinary superpower that clearly stands out to everyone, including yourself, it can be difficult to see what other people think is special about yourself.

Put yourself in someone else's shoes for a minute, particularly the shoes of someone who has a pretty decent opinion of you (we all have at least a few of those). Now that you're pretending to be someone else, what do you think that person admires about you?

Still struggling? Here are two alternative ways you could ask this question:

What do people consistently compliment you about?
When you hear multiple compliments about a particular skill, it's a pretty good indicator that skill stands out to others.

What do people often thank you for?
When people consistently thank you for something you do, they are often saying, *"I wasn't able to do that, but you were, so thanks!"*

People admire YOU for something. What do they see?

5. What do you do that makes a positive difference?

You have some talents that clearly make a positive difference in your life or the lives of others. Think about the things you do that result in an obvious improvement to something. Maybe it's a physical improvement in someone's life, such as when you build homes for Habitat for Humanity. It could be an improvement in someone's financial situation when you buy their groceries. You might lift someone's mood when you write them an encouraging note, or when you secretly pay for the coffee of the next person in line at Starbucks. Maybe you improve your own well-being when you sing, or paint, or build, or organize.

I don't know a single person who doesn't have some skills that make a positive difference. I'm betting you have a bunch.

6. What do you enjoy doing most in the whole world?
This one may seem obvious, but it's also easy to overlook. We don't always equate the things we enjoy the most with actual talents or skills, probably because we focus so much on the enjoyment part; we don't ever stop to dissect how we arrive there.

Think about the activities you enjoy the most. What are you doing in those activities? What talents or skills are you using when you're immersed in that enjoyment?

Being entertained doesn't count. Pure entertainment, such as watching a movie or attending a sporting event, is passive. You're not doing anything but watching.

However, if what you enjoy about movies or basketball games is taking specific people with you because you know they'll enjoy it, that's different. Then the focus isn't about being passively entertained, it's about you using entertainment to serve someone else.

A talent or activity doesn't have to serve someone else to qualify here, though. It might serve only you, and that's fine. What lights you up? What makes you feel great? What gives you immense satisfaction? It might be writing short stories or rock climbing or mowing the grass (don't laugh, that one is on my list). The point is you enjoy it, period.

THE TASK OR ROLE MAY (OR MAY NOT) BE THE SUPERPOWER

When you answer the questions...

What are you always doing?

What do people always ask you for help doing?

I DON'T KNOW A SINGLE PERSON WHO DOESN'T HAVE SOME SKILLS THAT MAKE A POSITIVE DIFFERENCE. I'M BETTING YOU HAVE A BUNCH.

What do you always feel compelled to volunteer for?

What do you do that other people admire?

What do you do that makes a positive difference?

What do you enjoy doing most in the world?

...the tasks or roles you identify may be your Ordinary Superpowers. Or they simply may be deeper clues or good indicators as to what your true Ordinary Superpowers are.

Your Ordinary Superpowers may be the task itself, but it could just be related to the task. For instance, if people always ask you to help them fix their computer, one of your Ordinary Superpowers might be *fixing computers*. There's just something about computers that you understand, and you have a real knack for rooting out the cause of the breakdown and fixing it. Done. End of story.

However, your Ordinary Superpowers could simply be showcasing themselves through certain tasks or activities. Using the same example from above: If you're great at fixing computers, it could be because your real superpower is *solving process-oriented problems,* or *recognizing patterns.* It could even be that you love *diving into a problem that most people shy away from,* even if you don't have any idea how to fix it (but somehow you always figure it out).

As you identify the tasks and roles you naturally perform (or feel compelled to perform), ask yourself which talents or skills you exercise when you perform those activities. Then, think about where else you use those talents or skills. *Do you use your problem-solving skill only when you fix computers, or do you frequently use it in other tasks or activities as well, such as rearranging the office for better efficiency or mediating arguments between family members?*

APPLY THE TEST TO BE SURE

As you identify skills, tasks, and roles from this thinking, you will undoubtedly have a decent-sized list in your head or even on paper (if you're taking notes). You may be thinking that there's no way everything on that list can be a superpower, and you're right. Whether the talents on your list are a God-given strength or a skill you've developed through experience, to identify which ones are Ordinary Superpowers, you will need to apply the Ordinary Superpower test to each item on your list:

1. It comes naturally to me.
2. Most people DON'T have this power.
3. It helps people.
4. I enjoy using it.

If it doesn't pass all four parts of the test, it's not one of your Ordinary Superpowers.

If you discover several items on your list pass the test, take your evaluation to another level. If you had to pick just three of the items, *which three pass the test with the most flying colors?* Which three MOST meet the criteria? Look at your list as objectively as you can. There may be items that you wish were your strongest Ordinary Superpowers, but they don't necessarily pass all four parts of the test as powerfully as some of the other items do.

If you're struggling, use the test again, but use each part of the test as a tie-breaker by rephrasing the test a little on parts 1, 3, and 4:

1. Which one(s) come MOST naturally to me?
2. Most people don't have this power.
3. Which one(s) help people the MOST?
4. Which one(s) do I enjoy using the MOST?

If you still struggle with narrowing down your list, share your list with someone who knows you well and who will be honest and straightforward with you. Don't be surprised if they point out your top three right away. Your strongest Ordinary Superpowers have a way of being obvious to the people around you, even if they're not so obvious to you.

LEVERAGE THE POWER OF FOCUS

Why is it so important to narrow down to your top three Ordinary Superpowers? Because the more focused you are, the more powerful you are (think laser beam vs. floodlight). That doesn't mean you can't exercise the other abilities on your big list, but you will always contribute the most and get the most fulfillment by focusing on your true top superpowers.

Need proof? Look at the top performers in any industry. Top scientists are typically not also world-class violin players. Elite athletes are rarely also Oscar-winning actors. CEOs are not typically also master chefs. These people usually contribute at such high levels not because they have a broad range of Ordinary Superpowers, but because they have a small, focused set of Ordinary Superpowers that they have learned how to maximize for incredible results.

As soon as you discover your Ordinary Superpowers, you'll be able to do that, too.

PROGRESS, NOT PERFECTION

Got your Ordinary Superpowers all nailed down? It's okay if you don't. Honest. If you've never thought about this stuff before, it can take some time to perform the necessary self-reflection to feel confident enough to say, *"Yes, absolutely! These are my Ordinary Superpowers!"*

Even during my retreats where we spend an entire morning on this step, some people nail their powers right away, while others have to live with the material for a bit longer before clarity sinks in. Both approaches work just fine.

There is no such thing as self-development perfection. In fact, that would be an oxymoron, wouldn't it? What we're after here is progress, not perfection. As fun as it might be to whip through this book so you can leave an amazingly positive review of it on Amazon, take your time with this, even if that means you need to pause for a day or two to think about what you're experiencing and learning through this journey.

When you feel like you have a bit of a grip on what your Ordinary Superpowers are, turn the page, and we'll take those babies out for a spin.

READY TO DISCOVER?
Download the companion workbook at
www.markhenson.me/superpowerextras

2

ACTIVATE

"IF WE CAN SERVE OTHERS, WE SHOULD SERVE. IF WE CAN TEACH, WE SHOULD TEACH. IF WE CAN ENCOURAGE OTHERS, WE SHOULD ENCOURAGE THEM. IF WE CAN GIVE, WE SHOULD BE GENEROUS. IF WE ARE LEADERS, WE SHOULD DO OUR BEST. IF WE ARE GOOD TO OTHERS, WE SHOULD DO IT CHEERFULLY."

(Romans 12:7–8) — Paul
(Apostle Superhero)

CHAPTER 5

GET CLEAR FIRST

Before you can fully activate your Ordinary Superpowers, it is extremely helpful to spend some time getting clear on what they are and how they work in your life. Once you've discovered them, understanding how you're already using them is one key to knowing how to apply them more proactively in the future.

Remember what your top two or three Ordinary Superpowers are? I hope so; it's only been a couple of pages since you discovered them! Let's dig a little deeper and find out just how super your Ordinary Superpowers are. I'll remind you (and keep reminding you) that they're likely more super than you think. This chapter will start to prove that to you because we'll look at how and where you're already using them, and the positive impact you're already having, much of which you probably haven't heard about or noticed!

HOW DO YOU ALREADY USE THEM?

When you use your Ordinary Superpowers, what is it that you're actually *doing*? When I say one of my Ordinary Superpowers is "exploring the new," it shows up in many different types of doing. Some examples include:

- Brainstorming marketing ideas with my team
- Having an idea for a blog post and writing it out to see if it works
- Seeing an interesting store/restaurant/roadside attraction on a road trip and stepping inside to check it out
- Reading new books
- Asking lots of questions when I'm coaching someone

- Playing with new technology
- Rearranging my furniture
- Meeting new people

I'm always more excited by exploring something new than settling into something familiar. Because this is one of my Ordinary Superpowers, I'm *compelled* to pursue these kinds of activities. It's automatic.

As you explore how you use each of your Ordinary Superpowers, you may be surprised at how many different activities you can list once you get the ball rolling. Don't give up if you struggle to come up with more than a few actions or activities that utilize your superpowers. While one or two activities may strongly leverage your Ordinary Superpowers, most abilities, talents, and skills often show up in many other places. For instance, my Ordinary Superpower of "exploring the new" obviously shows up in the act of brainstorming ideas. But it also shows up when I rearrange my furniture (which I do way more often than most people, by the way).

Could an Ordinary Superpower show up in only one or two activities in your life? It's possible, I suppose. In my experience, however, when you have a superpower, you can't help using it in many different ways. In fact, you often use it so automatically that you don't even realize you're using one of your Ordinary Superpowers until you stop to think about it. I'll be honest, I never connected rearranging my furniture with "exploring the new" until I starting making my list. But now I can see it so clearly that I wonder why I never noticed it before.

WHERE DO YOU USE THEM?

If you've been thinking of HOW you use your Ordinary Superpowers, you've probably also thought about WHERE you use them. If you can't help using your superpowers in many different ways, I guarantee you also use them in many different places. The big three places in most of our lives are work, home, and community.

It's helpful to explore each of these areas to see whether there are other ways you're already using your Ordinary Superpowers. Each area of our lives has multiple facets to it, and you may discover that you're using your superpowers in ways and places you've never realized before. Here are some questions to help you explore how you may be using them in some of the different facets of your life. Spend some time with these questions, and don't blow off the exercise if answers don't come to you right away. You may have to dig a little, or even brainstorm with someone who knows you well.

How do you use your Ordinary Superpowers...

At Work

...in your repetitive day-to-day activities?

...in your special projects?

...when working alone?

...when collaborating with others?

At Home

...in your duties or activities at home?

...in your relationships with friends, significant other, or extended family?

...in your parenting?

In Your Community

...to help your neighbors?

...to serve your church, PTA, or other organizations?

...in any charity work that you do?

WHAT IMPACT DO THEY HAVE?

If part of the criteria of Ordinary Superpowers is that they help people (including you), then using your superpower should result in some sort of positive impact, right? Different activities will have different levels of impact. For me, brainstorming ideas with my team positively impacts my business, and often ends up increasing revenue and/or profit. More money gives me and my team the ability to do even more fun things. Rearranging my furniture might not add to my retirement account, but it does add to the day-to-day enjoyment of my living environment. These two examples offer different levels of impact for sure, but both are positive.

For the list you've been making on paper or in your head, ask yourself: *"For each of the ways and places I use my Ordinary Superpowers, what is the positive*

WHEN WE USE OUR ORDINARY SUPERPOWERS, WE'RE NOT JUST CREATING POSITIVE ENERGY FOR OURSELVES. WHEN WE GENERATE POSITIVE ENERGY, IT POSITIVELY AFFECTS EVERYONE AROUND US.

impact that is created as the result?" It doesn't have to be *every* time you use it, but it should be *usually* or *often*.

Other ways to ask this question are:

> *What problems do my Ordinary Superpowers solve?*
>
> *What benefits do they provide to me or those around me?*
>
> *What advantages do they create for me or others?*
>
> *How do they help change things for the better (in any way, large or small)?*

HOW DO YOU FEEL WHEN YOU USE THEM?

One of the byproducts of Ordinary Superpowers is that when you use them, they give you pleasure on some level. You enjoy using them, and not just because of the impact they create or the positive results they generate. The sheer act of engaging your Ordinary Superpowers is fun for you.

To help reinforce how powerful your Ordinary Superpowers are for you, go back through your lists of <u>how</u> and <u>where</u> you use them, and think about how you <u>feel</u> when you use them in all those situations. *Fun, pleasure,* and *enjoyment* can mean many different things, depending on the activity and context. It might show up as a feeling of productivity or accomplishment. It could also just be a "thrill" kind of feeling that's hard to explain, but you know it when you feel it.

When I brainstorm with my team, I feel creative and confident. Writing a blog post gives me a feeling of completion and contribution. Reading new books makes me feel smarter. Rearranging my room gives me a feeling of lightness. These are all quite different feelings, but all good feelings to me.

The common result of any of the good feelings we experience — which we often call fun, pleasure, or enjoyment — could simply be called *positive energy.* What makes this even better is that when we use our Ordinary Superpowers, we're not just creating positive energy for ourselves. When we generate positive energy, it positively affects everyone around us. True positive energy expands outward, creating a ripple effect.

Negative energy can do that, too (in a negative way, of course). However, positive energy and negative energy can't occupy the same space at the same time. In fact, they repel each other. So the best way to keep negative energy as far away as possible is to do everything you can to generate positive energy. The good news is now you know you can create positive energy anytime you want by proactively engaging your Ordinary Superpowers.

Are your Ordinary Superpowers clearer to you now? It takes some effort to examine your activities and talents. Most people never take the time to live an examined life, so I applaud you for the work you're doing. I also hope you're feeling good about your powers and beginning to realize that you've likely only scratched the surface of what you can do with them. In the coming chapters, we'll talk more about how to proactively use your Ordinary Superpowers. We'll also talk about enhancing and multiplying them to create greater impact and exponentially greater positive energy in the world.

But first, we need to have an important conversation about passion.

CHAPTER 6

WHEN YOUR SUPER PASSIONS AREN'T YOUR SUPERPOWERS

You're now far enough into this journey to have an inkling of what your Ordinary Superpowers might be. At the least, you've started to narrow down your list.

You might even be questioning your superpowers at this point, especially if you don't think they match up to your greatest desires. That can be a difficult spot, and I believe it may be more common than most people think. That's why I think we need to pause here to talk about passions and how they relate to superpowers. Although the world tries to mesh passions and superpowers together, they're not the same thing. It is important to distinguish between the two, to understand whether they align, and if so, how.

Our current society unquestionably messes with our heads. We are constantly promised that if we follow our interests and passions, our lives will become all butterflies and unicorns. Some of the more common messages we are bombarded with include:

"Do what you love and the money will follow."

"Choose a job you love, and you'll never have to work a day in your life."

"Make your passion your priority."

You may also have had your eye on a job, role, or career that you believe will deliver the definition of success or fulfillment that we talked about in Chapter 3. Sometimes we see someone else in a particular role, and we want what they have, whether it's money, freedom, control, power, admiration, or an office with a killer view. Other times, we get a taste of that role, and we like it so much we just know we want more.

Or it can be a combination of all of the above. I chased a career in radio for more than a decade. When I was in 7th grade, two on-air personalities from a local radio station deejayed one of our awkward middle-school dances. I thought those DJs were the coolest people I'd ever seen, and they were having so much fun! Instantly, I knew what I wanted to do with the rest of my life, or at least the foreseeable future.

From that moment until the time I was 27 years old, I pursued a career in radio with a vengeance. I took a radio broadcasting class in high school and successfully lobbied for an independent study in radio my senior year. I joined the radio station staff at my college and became the general manager for two years. I worked at two of the top radio stations in Oklahoma City before I even graduated, and then several more in Lansing, Michigan and Columbus, Ohio after I got my degree.

I loved radio; I loved being on the air. I loved putting together my 7 p.m.–midnight show every day. I loved making commercials. I loved creating and running contests, promotions, and events, which eventually led two of the stations I worked for to add *Promotion Director* to my business card (which meant a ton of extra work for no extra money). I even loved the look and feel of a radio studio! In fact, I still get a shot of adrenaline when I see a microphone and a mixing board.

I was also a pretty good DJ. One of the stations I worked for achieved (and maintained) the highest 7 p.m.–midnight ratings in the whole city. Okay, it was Lansing, not Los Angeles, but, hey, for a few years I was a big deal among the 12- to 24-year-old demographic in Mid-Michigan.

Did I mention that during my last seven years in radio I got fired from three different radio stations? At the time, I thought it was just the way things happened in radio. In retrospect, I'm pretty sure it was the universe telling me I was play-

ONCE YOU DISCOVER
AN ORDINARY
SUPERPOWER, THEY
WILL CONTINUE
TO SERVE YOU FOR
THE REST OF YOUR
LIFE, NO MATTER
WHAT PASSIONS OR
PROFESSIONS APPEAR
IN YOUR PATH.

ing in the wrong sandbox. I was pretty young, and pretty thick in the head, so it took the universe three tries before I finally got the message.

Was I using my Ordinary Superpowers as a DJ and radio promotion director? Actually, I often was, I just didn't know it. Every day, I created a new show. I had no budget to work with, so everything had to be simple and creative. And I basically wrote and spoke into a microphone for a living. All of these things were embodiments of my Ordinary Superpowers: exploring new ideas, simplifying things, and communicating ideas through writing and speaking.

I certainly wasn't consciously focused on maximizing my Ordinary Superpowers at that time. I was simply chasing what I thought was my calling. Unfortunately, working in radio also forced me to engage in a lot of non-superpower activities as well, which eventually led to a fair amount of misery. It turned out that it wasn't my lifelong calling after all.

After the third painful firing, I wasn't quite so passionate about radio any more. It was the first time I had ever considered that there might be life and work outside of broadcasting. That was also the moment I embarked on my journey of self-discovery, personal improvement, and focusing more and more on my Ordinary Superpowers (long before I coined the name). It only took me 20 more years to realize what I was doing and finally figure out a way to help other people focus on their Ordinary Superpowers, too. Like I've said, thick in the head.

DON'T CONFUSE YOUR SUPER PASSIONS WITH YOUR SUPERPOWERS

I wanted to be in radio so badly that I convinced myself being a DJ was my superpower. After all, I was good at it, and I certainly loved my craft. Looking back on it now, though, I can see that my Ordinary Superpowers had nothing to do with radio; I was just applying my superpowers in that particular job. Over the next 20 years, I was able to apply them in several other roles in several different industries as a copywriter, information designer, business owner, writer, speaker, facilitator, and coach.

Turns out my Ordinary Superpowers of exploring new ideas, simplifying things, and communicating through writing and speaking have much broader and more diverse applications than just introducing the latest hit songs to teenagers.

There is nothing wrong with having passions, and I sincerely hope your Ordinary Superpowers align with your passions. That's the dream, and I think that's what all those "follow your passion" motivational quotes are trying to encourage. Be careful, though, of thinking your passions are your Ordinary Superpowers. They may be related, but they are also distinctly separate from each other.

Here's an easy way to look at it:

- Passions are your unique interests and desires.
- Ordinary Superpowers are your most remarkable talents and skills.

Another key observation is that your passions may, and often do, come and go. What you're passionate about at 25 is likely to be different than what you're passionate about at 55. But, your Ordinary Superpowers will always be your Ordinary Superpowers. Once you discover an Ordinary Superpower, it will continue to serve you for the rest of your life, no matter what passions or professions appear in your path. The best news is that when you understand your Ordinary Superpowers, you can pursue, explore, and enjoy your passions more effectively than ever.

You've now identified your Ordinary Superpowers and gained even more understanding of them by clarifying them and thinking about how they support and advance your passions.

By the way, you've performed magnificently so far, and that makes me happy. I can't stress enough how important this first step of the process is (Discovering your Ordinary Superpowers) to the overall goal of this book, which is to help you fully maximize your powers. Before I challenge you to *proactively* put your superpowers to use, though, I want you to first understand your Default Operating System.

CHAPTER 7

UNDERSTAND YOUR DEFAULT OPERATING SYSTEM

As you move toward using your Ordinary Superpowers more proactively, it is extremely helpful to know where you're starting from and what your "default" settings are — how you automatically move about your life, react to various situations, and deal with challenges that arise. It is also helpful to understand the "dark side" of our Ordinary Superpowers.

Inside every computer is a critical piece of software called the operating system. Microsoft Windows and Apple's operating systems are two of the most familiar computer operating systems. Operating systems are the default way the computers work. Everything a computer does, every piece of software you install, must run through that default operating system in order to work. Sure, there are some amazing software applications out there that can help us do incredible things, but I think the real hero is the operating system. It's a total workhorse, it helps everything else work better, and it is completely under-appreciated.

Your Ordinary Superpowers are kind of like your default operating system. They are always there in the background, ready to help. Since they're "always on," you probably use them often, but you mostly use them *reactively*. Since you don't really think about them (or at least, you didn't before now), you don't *proactively* put them to use. The good news is that even operating in default mode, your Ordinary Superpowers likely yield some pretty great results.

So if you're still struggling to identify what your top two or three Ordinary Superpowers are, think about what your default settings are. What abilities just come out of you no matter what? I'll give you a few examples from some of my current team members:

My Chief Reality Officer (his fun title for Operations Manager), Jason Messick, is a natural born researcher. One of his default settings is to gather information. He asks tons of questions, he searches the internet, he fills his head with facts, figures, and details. It's just what he does. This has resulted in many cost savings for our company as he finds better and cheaper alternatives for supplies. It also contributes to some pretty solid relationship-building with our clients, because he remembers things like kids' names and other important details about our clients.

My Director of Guest Happiness (in charge of reservations and guest relations), Leah Senecal, always takes 100% responsibility when she's involved in something. She takes care of every detail that crosses her path and never lets anything slip through the cracks. The result? Our clients trust her implicitly. In fact, if I answer the phone, they don't even want to talk to me — and I'm the *owner*. They want to talk to *her* because they just know she'll take care of whatever they need.

My wife, Eve (my most important team member for sure), naturally organizes things. Give her a project, and the first thing she does is make a list of everything that needs to be done. She wasn't trained in any special method of project management, she just does it without even thinking about it. To demonstrate how much of a list-maker she is, I have seen her write "make another list" on her current to-do list. No kidding. I tease her about it, but I love her for it because I am NOT a planner or a list-maker. If she didn't use her list-making powers, I'm pretty sure my life would collapse.

Each of these examples is what happens in each person's default mode, without even any real thought or effort (at least it doesn't feel like effort to that person). Imagine what will happen when you start to *proactively* use and improve on what already comes naturally to you.

When you make that shift, you finally start to tap into the true power of your Ordinary Superpowers.

BEWARE THE DARK SIDE

I don't want to make a big deal about this, and I don't want to scare you, but your Ordinary Superpowers likely have a bit of evil in them. That dark side shows up when we overuse our powers, or we use them in the wrong place at the wrong time, or when we're oblivious to how our powers affect other people. It's bound to happen, especially since our Ordinary Superpowers are our default operating system.

You've witnessed this before, I'm sure. For example, some people have the Ordinary Superpower of using humor to connect with people. That doesn't fly so well when they're in the middle of an argument or attending a funeral. However, since it is part of their default operating system, they might use humor at inappropriate times if they're not careful.

In my team, here's how the dark side may show up:

If Jason doesn't set a deadline for his fact-finding, he may keep digging, and digging, and digging. That's great for gathering lots of info, not so great if you need to make a decision quickly.

If Leah doesn't set some boundaries on her responsibility, she might take work home on a regular basis or end up working on her days off. I know that sounds like a dream employee to some managers, but we all know that behavior inevitably leads to burnout.

If Eve overshares her giant to-do lists with other people, she could completely stress those people out (maybe even people she's married to) because I — I mean THEY — get easily overwhelmed by giant to-do lists.

Likewise, I've come to realize that some people don't enjoy brainstorming like I do. They don't want to explore every option and new idea; they just want a quick answer or solution. If I try to generate ideas with a person like that, I might actually see his/her head explode, and nobody wants to see that, right?

Managing the dark side of your Ordinary Superpowers probably involves a straightforward solution, but that doesn't mean that it's always easy to do.

That's because managing the dark side of your Ordinary Superpowers often means turning off your superpowers temporarily (or at least turning them down significantly for a bit or using them in the background). Fair warning: this can be like trying to turn off a blender with no "off" switch while simultaneously discovering it's hard-wired to the national power grid.

One strategy for doing this is to build awareness of how your powers affect the people around you and adjust accordingly. Watch for negative reactions when you suspect you've crossed over to the dark side. An even more direct strategy would be to ask people straight up how they feel when the knob on your Ordinary Superpowers is turned all the way to 11.

I know it's weird to think that something that is so much a part of your winning formula in life could have potentially damaging side effects. Don't sweat it, though. Awareness is the key, and now that you're thinking about it, your awareness has already increased.

And as you proactively use your Ordinary Superpowers more, you'll begin to naturally know where and when to use your powers — and when not to as well.

CHAPTER 8

PROACTIVELY PUT YOUR ORDINARY SUPERPOWERS TO USE

Have you ever known somebody who always seems to operate "in the zone"? Not only do they seem to do whatever it is they do effortlessly, they also get great results, and they appear to thoroughly enjoy what they do. Their chosen profession doesn't matter, how they operate within their life does. If you examine these people closely, you'll see them frequently using their Ordinary Superpowers in many aspects of their lives.

People who operate in the zone don't do it accidentally. They are intentional, purposeful, and proactive about using their superpowers to create the results they desire. They intentionally hack their default operating system, and they not only figure out *how* to use their powers more, but also *where* they can use them to make a positive difference. In this chapter, you'll learn how to do this as well, just like my friend Dan has done.

When I first met Dan Putt, he was a young, fresh-faced college student at The Ohio State University. My wife joked that he looked like an Abercrombie model (to which I would always reply, "Settle down, Mrs. Robinson"). But right away I knew Dan was more than the handsome boy next door. He has the laid-back energy of a surfer (even though he is from Ohio) and he has an impressive ability to connect with all kinds of people. He is passionate about exploring and experimenting with business ideas. In fact, while he was still in school, Dan launched a business reselling used PDA devices (think smart phones without the phone part) on overseas eBay sites. After school, he explored and/or launched several other businesses and eventually co-founded Reboot, a coaching company that helps tech entrepreneurs deal with the internal ups and downs of entrepreneurship and being a CEO.

Dan's greatest Ordinary Superpower is *curiosity*. He's curious about new ideas. He's curious about how to make things better. He's curious about people, their stories, and their capabilities. If something piques his interest that he doesn't understand or know how to pursue, his curiosity kicks in and he seeks knowledge, finds people who know more than he does, and experiments until he figures things out.

Dan doesn't just apply his curiosity to exploring and starting businesses. Although he didn't necessarily realize this until I shared the concept of Ordinary Superpowers with him, Dan *proactively applies* curiosity in every area of his life. He was curious about what it would be like to live in New York City, so he moved there to find out. After he arrived, he started hearing about this venture capitalist named Jerry Colonna who had a reputation as a phenomenal coach and mentor to entrepreneurs. Dan became curious about Jerry and whether Jerry would meet with him, so he contacted him. The short story is now, years later, Jerry and Dan are partners in a successful venture that is making a positive difference in the lives of others.

Dan is currently exploring the world with even greater curiosity through the eyes of his first child and will no doubt pass along the Ordinary Superpower of curiosity to the next generation.

While Dan is a great example of someone who proactively uses an Ordinary Superpower in many different ways, I've also encountered some people who clearly have an Ordinary Superpower, but seem to be using it in only one area of their life. It's as if they haven't yet discovered their remarkable talent could have multiple applications.

I have a cordless drill. Of course I use it to drill holes when I need to. I *could* also use it to buff my car, clean clogged drains, and strip paint from various objects. In fact, there are at least 87 other things I could use my drill for besides creating small, perfect holes in wood three or four times a year.

Just as I need to remember how useful my cordless drill could be in many different ways and places, I also need to remember that each of my superpowers likely has at least 87 other potential uses as well.

One of my greatest hopes for this book is that it will help you recognize your Ordinary Superpowers, completely own them, and use them in many different ways.

STOP OPERATING IN DEFAULT MODE

Up until this point, your Ordinary Superpowers have been operating in "default" mode. That means they only kicked in when you found yourself — through no real effort of your own — in situations where you just sort of naturally used your powers when you needed to, because you were there and you had nothing better to do.

Now that you've started to gain appreciation for the unique combination of abilities, talents, and skills that only you have, it's time to start activating them for even greater good. I'm asking you right now to start proactively looking for opportunities that need your superpower skill set.

Caution: when you start to proactively use your Ordinary Superpowers, you are incredibly likely to start getting results you didn't expect. Good ones. Projects moving along faster than ever. Or connecting with people in a deeper, more meaningful way. You might start receiving big high-fives for stuff you do that you think is rather ordinary. I'm not saying you'll get to be the Grand Marshall of the Macy's Thanksgiving Day Parade, but I'm not going to rule it out, either.

HOW TO BE MORE PROACTIVE WITH YOUR POWERS:

I'm trying not to overdo it with the "how to" stuff in this book, but there are a couple of places where I think it's helpful. This is one of them. Here are three steps to take that will help you use your powers more proactively:

1. Be Clear about Your Ordinary Superpowers.
We've covered this already, but it is the #1 thing you need to do (hence the repetition).

2. Pay Attention.

As you move about your day, look up from your laptop or phone once in a while. Does anyone need your special brand of help? When you meet with people, listen for the challenges and opportunities that could benefit from your Ordinary Superpowers. You might find out the person who sits right next to you could use your assistance, they just didn't know to ask (or didn't want to bother you).

Have you ever been working on a computer and someone wanders by and says, "Hey, you know if you used the XYZ shortcut instead of the ABC one, it might work better." And then you sit there, dumbfounded, because you didn't even know about the XYZ shortcut, and you ask yourself, *"Holy crap, why has no one ever told me about the XYZ shortcut before?"* That's what everyone who doesn't have your superpowers is like — they probably don't know what they don't know. They might not even see the same problems that you can see. So don't be afraid to offer your help.

3. Test the Waters.

Learning how to proactively use your Ordinary Superpowers may take a little time. Problems you thought were a perfect fit for your talents might not be, while problems that you blow off thinking you can't help with might be an ideal match for your powers. The only way to know is to take your powers out for a spin every so often. Please don't look just for "perfect" opportunities, especially not at first. Perfectionism is an excuse for procrastination. And the world needs you to use your unique abilities as soon as possible, as often as possible. Understood?

Once you begin to use your Ordinary Superpowers more proactively, you'll gain a deeper understanding about what you're truly capable of and what situations (and people) your powers best serve. When you get to that point, you can start choosing when to activate your powers for the greatest good. The greatest good doesn't have to be world-changing or earth-shattering. Sometimes the greatest good may be literally helping a little old lady cross the street or complimenting the cashier at the grocery store on her wicked-awesome fingernail polish.

WHERE, WHEN, WHAT, WHOM?

Only you can determine where, when, for what and for whom to proactively engage your Ordinary Superpowers. That said, there are three key circles most of us operate within every day that hold a wealth of potential for our powers.

CAUTION: WHEN YOU START TO PROACTIVELY USE YOUR ORDINARY SUPERPOWERS, YOU ARE INCREDIBLY LIKELY TO START GETTING RESULTS YOU DIDN'T EXPECT. GOOD ONES.

Work

We spend our largest chunk of time at work (100,000+ hours in our adult life if we're lucky). It makes sense that we would want to maximize our contribution there. Truly fortunate people hold or create jobs that take full advantage of their Ordinary Superpowers. You have way more control over this part of your life than many people believe. America is *always* abundant with opportunity (yes, even when the economy is down). Many other parts of the world are as well.

Look around your workplace. Look beyond your job title and past your narrowly focused to-do list. Who can you help? What projects NEED you? What could you easily take over with your talents that other people probably hate doing? *Remember, what you're phenomenal at doing, most people aren't. What you love doing, other people don't.* That screams opportunity! Actually, now that I think about it, it *whispers* opportunity. If it screamed, you wouldn't have to pay as much attention. It also might freak you out a little.

Home

Even though we may spend the most *time* working, the most *important part* of our life for most of us is our home life. Unless you're THE scientist who is about to cure cancer. Then I could make an argument that work is kind of important, too. But for most of us, home wins.

Your spouse, kids, parents, siblings, friends — anyone you consider to be part of your family in some way — they're pretty special to you, yes? If you could make their life better and easier, you'd do it in a heartbeat, yes? If you proactively activated your Ordinary Superpowers more at home, this would automatically happen, yes?

It can be tricky to identify how you can use your Superpowers at home. At home you're just mom (or dad). You're just honey or sweetie or whatever your spouse calls you. And those titles come with all the roles and responsibilities associated with them. It doesn't feel as though there is much flexibility in the talents required to do the job. However, if you think proactively about your powers and how they might help you do your "home jobs" even better, you'll find many ways to use them to serve the people you care about the most.

Community

Work and home are easy. Community takes a little more work for some of us. Sure, there are people who are always helping everybody, always volunteering for the PTA, or always working to save the baby seals. I admire those people, but I'm not one of them. It's not that I don't want to help. I do. It's just that as a business owner, I have a tendency to put on blinders to everything but my job and my family. I use the excuse that I don't have time, but if I'm being honest, I just don't like to waste my time being a warm body.

One of the biggest complaints about volunteering I hear is lack of organization. Just because a person or group has a passion to make a difference doesn't mean they have the skills to do it. The results are often half-baked efforts to rally people around a cause or project. The prevailing philosophy states, "If we just have enough people involved, the problem will get solved." In my experience, that is simply not true, unless the problem you're trying to solve is filling a room with a bunch of warm bodies doing a mediocre job of volunteering.

If the philosophy shifted to getting the RIGHT people involved, then I'd wholeheartedly agree. The RIGHT people would have the Ordinary Superpowers needed to get the job done. Each person involved would be able to perform their piece of the project efficiently and effectively, and we could all go home a lot earlier because we'd totally rock the project.

Here's the problem: organizers/leaders (and participants) of many community events, projects, or challenges don't understand this concept or don't know how to make it happen (i.e., how to get the right people in the right seats on the right bus, to borrow a concept from *Good To Great* author Jim Collins).

But YOU do. At least I hope you do now. When you know how you contribute at your highest level, help the most people, and get the most fulfillment, you can look for opportunities in your community to do just that.

You're no doubt already making a list of how, where, and when you can use your Ordinary Superpowers more proactively. You also realize no matter what your powers are, there are countless opportunities to activate your Ordinary Superpowers and no shortage of people/organizations that would LOVE for you to step up and do your thing. You don't have to be a warm body. You can be a body that's fired up and focused. When you plug in where you can contribute the most, you'll find a whole new level of energy and enjoyment in community service.

BEWARE THE NON-SUPERPOWERS

I'm going to tell you something you probably don't want to hear, even if (maybe especially if) you already know it.

You waste a lot of time.

Everyone does.

Okay, maybe a monk in the mountains of Tibet doesn't waste much time. But the rest of us waste a boatload of time every day. We don't mean to. In fact, we actually think we're productive. But, in reality, we're only productive *sometimes*. The rest of the time we're just busy. And I'm not even sure "productive" is all it's cracked up to be.

Believe it or not, we waste most of our time in activities in which we have a fair amount of ability or skill. In this chapter, I'll explain more about how and why we focus on the wrong things, and I'll give you a way to honestly evaluate how you're spending your time so you can start shifting your focus back to where you make the biggest difference.

SURE, YOU'RE PRODUCTIVE, BUT WHAT ARE YOU PRODUCING?

Here's what most people consider productive: getting things done. Making progress on projects, clearing out their inbox, checking off some/most/all of their to-do list. There is a multi-gazillion dollar industry that is fueled by our desire to be more productive today than we were yesterday. There are countless

books, seminars, webinars, coaches, consultants and organizing systems that promise to cure you of the disease of unproductivity. We trade our hard-earned money, sacrifice our valuable time and volunteer our already fractured attention for these promises, and yet...

We keep finding ourselves feeling like we're still not as productive as we *should* be. I detest that word, *should*. It is pure evil and needs to be stricken from the dictionary and burned at the stake. There is no other word in the English language with such power to make you feel horrible about yourself.

Let me propose an idea: *your productivity isn't the problem*. *What* you're producing is, and possibly *how* you're producing it is, too.

Peter Drucker was THE guru of management thinking in the second half of the 20th century. There is one gem of a quote from him that stands out to me as a bright, shining beacon of truth:

"There is nothing so useless as doing efficiently that which should not be done at all."

BAM! That one hits me in the face, painfully hard, every time I read it. And rightfully so.

It is so easy for me to slip into "productivity mode." I do it so I can feel like I'm actually accomplishing something. I can almost convince myself that productivity equals contribution. Most of the time when I'm in productivity mode, I'm engaging my "pretty good" talents and skills, NOT the remarkable ones that are my true superpowers.

For example, I'm pretty good at simple graphic design. I can easily throw my energy into designing a web page, a blog graphic, or workshop materials. I can just as easily convince myself that I'm doing good, necessary work for my business. I enjoy doing this kind of work. It's creative, artistic, and results in a useful, tangible "thing." But if I'm honest with myself and apply the four-part Ordinary Superpower test to graphic design, here's what I have to admit:

1. It comes naturally to me. *Kinda.*
2. Most people DON'T have this power. *Actually, in my circle I have many friends who are WAY better graphic designers than I am (they have degrees and everything).*
3. It helps people. *I could make a case.*

4. I enjoy using it. *Absolutely.*

So, apparently graphic design is NOT one of my Ordinary Superpowers because it fails one part of the test pretty horrifically. I somehow continue to let it seduce me anyway.

Every minute I spend doing graphic design is another minute I'm not exploring new ideas and places, simplifying things, and communicating ideas through writing and speaking — my TRUE Ordinary Superpowers.

Does this mean I can never do graphic design again? Nah. I can still do graphic design, but I need to understand its place in my life, and prioritize it accordingly. I can still do it when I need some quick graphic design on-the-fly. I can do it when I just want to produce something, or when I need a creative distraction.

However, I know that if I let go of this activity even *50 percent of the time that I do it now,* two things will happen: I'll have a ton more time to focus on activities that allow me to contribute at my highest level AND I'll end up with higher quality graphic design. I know this is true, because whenever I delegate a design project to a "real" designer, I end up smiling and shaking my head at myself when they deliver a product far better than what I would have designed. My attempts at graphic design look like kindergarten drawings by comparison.

I can almost hear you defending yourself in your head: *"But I can't JUST use my superpowers and nothing else. I still have to do all those other things."*

Do you? Do you, really?

I get it. There are things you have to do. You have to pay the bills, you have to do the laundry, and somebody needs to make mac 'n cheese for the kids or they will die. You don't have the money right now to hire a bookkeeper, send all your clothes to the laundry, or employ a private chef who specializes in mac 'n cheese cuisine.

I'm not talking about all the stuff you absolutely HAVE to do just to live your life. I'm talking about an activity (or two or three) you find yourself repeatedly sucked into because you're pretty good at it, and you might even enjoy, but it's not one of your Ordinary Superpowers.

That said, I'll also challenge the idea that the list of things we feel like we *have* to do is pretty bogus. Many of the things on that list are *wants*, not *needs*, and I'll prove it to you with the following sentence:

There has never been a single coroner's report that listed "unfolded laundry" as the cause of death. I'll admit, I didn't fact-check that statement. However, I feel pretty confident of its accuracy.

TAKE A GOOD LOOK AT HOW YOU SPEND YOUR TIME

If you want to test yourself, try this activity: Make a list of EVERY activity you do in the course of a week. If you want the PhD in this area, review an entire month. Take a good look at how you spend your time, then ask yourself two questions:

1. How many of my activities are truly wants versus needs?

2. How often do I use my Ordinary Superpowers in any form?

Fair warning — this activity can make you sigh out loud repeatedly and bludgeon yourself silly with phrases like, *"I should stop doing these things,"* or *"I should be using my Ordinary Superpowers so much more."* We've already discussed how evil that *should* word is. The point of the activity isn't to make you feel bad about yourself (although it probably will, at least temporarily). It's to wake you up and make you more aware of how you spend your time.

Realizing how you spend your time (and where you might be wasting it) is absolutely crucial in your journey to maximizing your Ordinary Superpowers. It is the #1 thing that will free you up to be able to Activate your Ordinary Superpowers even more than you already do.

Now that you've taken the first step of Discovering your Ordinary Superpowers and the second step of Activating them, it's time to lift your foot again to take the next step. This one isn't just a step forward, though — it's a step *up*. I'm a firm believer in the idea that you can always improve your powers, no matter how great they are. So, ready for a little Enhancement?

READY TO ACTIVATE?
Download the companion workbook at
www.markhenson.me/superpowerextras

STEP

3

ENHANCE

"ONE REASON SO FEW OF US ACHIEVE WHAT WE TRULY WANT IS THAT WE NEVER DIRECT OUR FOCUS; WE NEVER CONCENTRATE OUR POWER. MOST PEOPLE DABBLE THEIR WAY THROUGH LIFE, NEVER DECIDING TO MASTER ANYTHING IN PARTICULAR."

Tony Robbins
(Personal Development Superhero)

CHAPTER 10

YOU'RE STRONGER THAN YOU THINK

So you've got superpowers, you have a pretty good idea what they are, and you're keeping a proactive eye open for how to use them. That's a great start. But there's so much more you can do with your superpowers.

How? By enhancing them, improving them, and mastering them.

There was a TV show in the '70s called *The Six Million Dollar Man*. The main character, Steve Austin, was an astronaut. If you know anything about astronauts, they're pretty amazing. They're the best of the best. They're highly intelligent and incredibly physically fit. They're resilient and strong in mind, body, and spirit. Back in the early days, many of them graduated from top-gun fighter pilot to rocket commanders. Needless to say, they're badass in every way.

So, back to the story of Steve Austin. Through no fault of his own (badass, remember?) he crashed his spaceship. He was a hot mess, basically a half-inch from death's door. But the government believed in Steve, so they not only saved his life and patched him up, they took his rehab to a whole new level. They spent *six million dollars* to upgrade the man. The intro of the show told the whole story:

"Steve Austin, astronaut. A man barely alive. Gentlemen, we can rebuild him. We have the technology. We have the capability to make the world's first bionic

man. Steve Austin will be that man. Better than he was before. Better... stronger... faster."

When Steve woke up from surgery, he had two bionic legs, a bionic arm, a bionic eye, and likely some other random bionic parts the writers reserved to tell us about in later episodes (but only if needed to keep us glued to the TV). I don't remember the specifics, but I do recall that before Steve could become the ultimate government operative and save the world on a weekly basis, he had to *learn how to use his better, stronger, faster body parts.* I'm sure he jumped a little too high the first time and landed in a tree, probably accidentally crushed a coffee cup or two, and saw a few things with his bionic eye that he wished he could un-see.

At this point in the book, you're a lot like Steve Austin, only (hopefully) you haven't lost three of your limbs and an eye in a horrific spaceship accident. But I'm hoping you *have* awakened a bit and discovered you have talents and skills that are more super than you thought. Now that you've discovered them, you might even feel like they're strangely *new*, in a good way. You've never looked at your Ordinary Superpowers this way before. You've started to use them more, and now you're wondering just what else you can achieve with them. And you might be wondering, *"Just how strong ARE my new bionic parts anyway?"*

My answer to that question is, *"Let's find out!"*

The chapters in this section will show you how to enhance your Ordinary Superpowers so you can maximize the "bionics" you're carrying around with you right now.

By the way, I know you're wondering how much it would cost to create a bionic man like Steve Austin today. Thirty-three million dollars. I know, I looked it up, which has convinced me that somebody's Ordinary Superpower is finding random facts about vintage TV shows, making them relevant to the modern day, and posting them on the internet.

CHAPTER II

"POWER UP"

If you thought that discovering and activating was all you needed to do to maximize your Ordinary Superpowers, I have news for you. The first two steps are only the beginning, like learning to play basic chords on a guitar. Sure, you can strum a few songs, but you're no Jimi Hendrix — yet. Now that you have the basics down, it's time to shift your focus to taking your powers to the next level.

"But these are my SUPERPOWERS," you say. "Is it even possible to improve them?" I don't know why, but I imagine you saying that with your fists on your hips, wearing your cape, and holding your chin high in the air as you speak.

It is possible to improve your Ordinary Superpowers. In fact, there are several ways of going about it that we'll cover in the next few pages.

A GIANT OF AN EXAMPLE

It's no secret to the people around me that Tony Robbins is one of my longtime idols. In fact, I give Tony a mountain of credit for the success and happiness that I've found in my life overall. Like many people, I was first exposed to Tony via his late-night infomercials that sold his *Personal Power* cassettes (yes, I said cassettes).

Although I was captivated by this guy who seemed larger than life and more optimistic than any human being I'd ever met, I wasn't even slightly tempted to buy the program simply *because* those infomercials played at 2 a.m. I would laugh at all the "losers" who were suckered into buying the program because they were up at 2 a.m. eating Cheetos in their underwear wondering why their life wasn't going the way they wanted it to.

Then it dawned on me that the only reason I was seeing those infomercials was because *I was one of those people.* I wasn't totally desperate, but I did want to "play bigger" and create a better life for myself and the people around me. I also may or may not have consumed a bag or two of Cheetos late at night.

I still didn't buy the cassettes, though.

I DID eventually buy his book, *Awaken the Giant Within*, which was the first self-help book I ever purchased or read. I burned through it, eating it up like a secret stash of Halloween candy. It's safe to say I've read hundreds of books since then, and I can say without a doubt that none have impacted me as powerfully as that one did. I recently re-read major portions of that book and, aside from some dated references, it still holds up.

I told you all of that to tell you this: Tony Robbins is one of the best public speakers on the planet. At 6' 7", he's a commanding physical presence for sure, but I've seen many gigantic pro athletes who can't string together a proper sentence. I suspect Tony had some natural ability in the speaking area, but there isn't a single speaker alive who *started out* with the ability to engage and entertain a stadium full of people. His ability to communicate and connect comes from one place: practice and improvement. He even has an acronym he uses to describe it: CANI — Constant And Never-ending Improvement — which he has definitely applied to his speaking superpowers.

When Tony was first starting out, he had a theory that if a good speaker spoke, say, 10 times a year, and it took that speaker 10 years to become an excellent speaker, then simply spending more time speaking would help one become good much faster. So Tony figured if he spoke 100 times in a year, he would gain the equivalent of 10 years' worth of experience and improvement in a fraction of the time (one-tenth, to be exact). Of course, he's spoken thousands of times since then and keeps getting better.

HOW TO POWER UP YOUR ORDINARY SUPERPOWERS

A myth that too many people buy into is *you can't improve a superpower*. OF COURSE YOU CAN. Here are some ways you can "power up" your Ordinary Superpowers. By the way, you can improve just about any ability, talent, or skill this way, not just the super ones.

Use Them Every Day

Did you ever take a foreign language class in school? My wife took eight years of Spanish throughout high school and college. Know how much Spanish she

A MYTH THAT TOO MANY PEOPLE BUY INTO IS *YOU CAN'T IMPROVE A SUPERPOWER.* OF COURSE YOU CAN.

can speak today? Nada. She never used it, so not only did she never improve her ability to use the language, she actually *lost* her ability. Oh, she retained a few words and phrases, but not even enough to order a decent enchilada dinner. Me? I only took one semester of Español, and that was in 7th grade. I will definitely die of starvation if I am ever stranded in Mexico.

The concept of *"use it or lose it"* also applies to Ordinary Superpowers. Anything that doesn't get used tends to atrophy, weaken, and even disappear over time. We could also say *"use it, or accept the fact that you won't have as much impact as you could have."* Like a pile of money, if it's just sitting there, it doesn't do any good. For money to grow, you have to put it to use by investing it wisely or spending it to build something valuable.

The MORE you use your powers, however, the STRONGER they will get. When you use them, they get better, stronger, and faster (like the Six Million Dollar Man, but without the painful surgery). The stronger they get, the more they help people, and the more you'll enjoy using them. We LIKE to do stuff we're good at doing, but we LOVE to do stuff we're great at doing. Right?

Learn More about Your Powers
This shouldn't come as a shock to you, but you're not the only person on the planet with your Ordinary Superpowers. You *may* be the only person with your *exact combination* of powers, but there's a better-than-average chance that someone shares at least one of your remarkable talents — and has written a book about it. Or an article or blog post. Or filmed a YouTube video. Or created a workshop, class, or seminar.

Find those people, articles, posts, videos, workshops, classes, etc., and read them, buy them, experience them. Do a quick search of Amazon, Audible, or the entire internet, and they'll turn up. This is the absolute easiest way to begin to enhance your superpowers — learn from people who are using them differently or better than you are.

As you search for examples, information, and instruction, don't necessarily limit your learning to one specific topic. You may find great information in *related topics*, too. One of my Ordinary Superpowers is simplifying things. If I search for ways to simplify, I can find tons of information. However, if I expand my search to related topics like "minimalism" and "decluttering," I might find a whole new batch of info and resources. And, believe me, I have.

If one of your powers is naturally creating win-win situations, you could study negotiation tactics, mediation, or the science of influence to learn even more.

If one of your powers is inspiring others through poetry, you could find poetry-writing workshops, writing or blogging conferences, and attend poetry readings to be inspired by other poets. You might also study advertising copywriting or writings about food or nature, which are often quite descriptive and poetic.

If one of your powers is fact-finding, you could study information-gathering techniques or research methodologies, or take classes in library sciences. You could also study criminology or psychology.

Not every idea, tool, technique, etc., will apply to you, and that's okay. With any learning, especially the self-propelled learning you'll do to improve your Ordinary Superpowers, take what works for you, and be content with leaving the rest behind. You don't have to know everything, or apply every idea, to practice constant and never-ending improvement. You just have to keep learning.

Seek Out Role Models
Some of the people you will discover by learning more about your Ordinary Superpowers will naturally become role models for you. If one of your powers is helping the helpless, someone who founded a charity organization might become a role model for you, even if you never meet them. Is managing teams one of your powers? You might consider patterning yourself after another successful manager you discover, or perhaps a championship-winning basketball coach.

Sometimes we're lucky enough to find people who love to share their ideas through writing and speaking. Reading books or blogs and watching videos on YouTube are great ways to follow role models from afar. In my experience, when people write books or blogs, they often share their most useful tips and most powerful advice in those resources. If you've got a good library nearby, you don't even have to buy the book!

On the flip side, beware the "experts" who give a tiny bit of information, then want you to buy the rest via their online product or seminar. So many of these people are trying to profit on a one-hit success or limited experience. I always look for people who have been using their Ordinary Superpowers for years, not months. Yes, I know, Tony Robbins makes his living by selling online products and seminars. But he has also written fairly thick books, and if you pay attention to how much stuff he puts out for free, you'll see that he's generous with his knowledge, experience, and expertise. Look for role models like him.

Look immediately around you for mentors, too. There may be people in your circle of friends and acquaintances who share your superpowers and whom you may be able to learn a great deal from.

My cousin Mike is an outdoorsman with a rugged, manly beard and everything. He once spent 10 days backcountry hiking and camping in Alaska. He regularly climbs below the surface of the earth to explore caves (why he does this, I have no idea). He appreciates nature more than anyone I know, and he writes the most amazing Facebook posts about what he sees and experiences in nature every day. Believe me, if I ever need a mentor in anything related to exploring, experiencing, or observing the great outdoors, Mike's my man.

Almost certainly within the community you live in, there are potential mentors of every kind. Tools such as email, LinkedIn, and Facebook make facilitating introductions to people you want to meet quick, easy, and painless. If you're too timid to reach out to people you don't know (or even ones you do) because you think you'll be bothering them, relax. Most people are extremely flattered and willing to mentor someone who asks nicely. Heck, I'll meet just about anybody for coffee if they ask nicely. If they're paying for the coffee, they don't even have to be that nice.

Hire a Coach

A mentor, like the ones mentioned above, could be a coach. But a coach doesn't necessarily have to be a mentor. To me, a mentor is someone who has experience that you don't have yet. Mentors share stories and provide advice from their personal journey. A coach is someone with expertise in observation, correction, and improvement. They present options on how to move toward what you want. A coach can also help you navigate around obstacles and point out where you may be your own obstacle.

Coaching is definitely a skill, and when I engage a coach, I always look for one who has coaching as one of their Ordinary Superpowers. It doesn't matter whether I'm hiring them for an "official" coaching relationship or I'm just meeting them for breakfast to get some objective advice. I want someone who will naturally coach me; they just automatically do it. That's way different, by the way, from the kind of person who just can't help giving unsolicited advice. I actually try to NOT have breakfast with those people if I can help it, even if they're buying.

Even if your superpowers are *extraordinary*, you can still benefit from coaching. I once saw Tiger Woods on a tournament practice round, during the *peak* of his golf career, working with his coach on the course. At that moment in time, he was *unquestionably* the best player alive, and he was *still* coachable. I watched, with complete fascination, as his coach observed Tiger's swing, then moved his elbow and pushed his head down slightly. Tiger nodded in agreement, knowing his coach saw what he couldn't see. I only watched him work with his coach for one hole, but I learned a lesson that I will remember for the rest of my life: even when you're the best in the whole world, you can still improve — if you're willing to be coached.

One final piece of advice when it comes to finding a coach: you usually get what you pay for. Free coaching might seem great, but there's no real commitment on your part or the part of whoever is coaching you. I'm a big believer in hiring a coach, and hiring the absolute best coach you can afford. I know that when I spend good money on something, I tend to pay more attention because I want to make sure I'm not wasting my money. The more I pay, the higher my expectations are, too, so it holds their feet to the fire as well.

Hiring a coach is one of the best ways to help you enhance your powers. It's also a great way to figure out what your weaknesses are. Although some weaknesses are pretty obvious, sometimes we can be blind to things we didn't know were getting in the way of our success.

So, still think you can't improve your Ordinary Superpowers? I'm guessing you're now on board with the idea that there are several things you can do to intentionally create more positive change in your life, the lives of others, and the world around you.

I hit on this briefly a moment ago, but as we continue to build on our strengths, there's something else we need to pay attention to as well: our weaknesses. We don't necessarily like to think about our weaknesses, and we'd sweep them under the rug if we could. If we do that, though, they'll still be there under the rug, and we'll continue to trip over them, won't we? The final chapter in this section is dedicated to dealing with your weaknesses head-on so they stop interfering with your superpowers (and your success).

YOU DON'T HAVE TO KNOW EVERYTHING, OR APPLY EVERY IDEA, TO PRACTICE CONSTANT AND NEVER-ENDING IMPROVEMENT. YOU JUST HAVE TO KEEP LEARNING.

CHAPTER 12

MINIMIZE YOUR WEAKNESSES & AVOID YOUR KRYPTONITE

I debated whether to put this chapter in the book or not, because I'm not a big fan of focusing on your weaknesses. I believe you get the biggest bang for your buck by focusing on your strengths.

That said, we all have weaknesses, and it would be foolish to ignore them, especially if they are getting between us and what we want to achieve. The key is recognizing which weaknesses are worth improving, and which you should decide to accept as weaknesses.

Did I just give you permission to let some weaknesses be weaknesses? Yes, I did. We can't be great at everything, and we have a finite amount of time and energy to spend, so it makes sense to spend our time and energy on what will allow us to have the most positive impact. It will take a little more self-evaluation to know which weaknesses are causing noise in your life, and which ones are so debilitating that you consider them your own personal Kryptonite. Of course, a few strategies to help minimize your weaknesses and avoid your Kryptonite would be helpful, so we'll talk about those as well.

A CASE FOR MINIMIZING WEAKNESSES

I've always been great at getting ideas off the ground and getting projects start-ed. However, I've never been great at *managing* those ongoing projects or pro-cesses. For a long time, I thought, *"If I could just get better as a manager, my life would be so much easier and my business would run better and grow faster."* I read books, I attended management and leadership conferences, I subscribed to blogs on managing and productivity. I spent a significant amount of time and energy (and money, now that I think about it) trying to improve my manage-ment skills. The result? I got maybe 5% better as a manager, which means I still sucked, just 5% less. Looking back, it was a pretty bad investment.

What would have been more effective would have been to spend my *time and energy* on improving my ability to get things started, and spend my *money* hir-ing someone else to manage ongoing projects and processes. This may sound like a dilemma unique to entrepreneurs or small business owners, but it's not. I see people in all walks of life, in all types of industries, in every level of position, facing this same struggle every day.

You can't always hire away your weaknesses, so you must learn how to mini-mize them when you need to.

Think of your talents as a multi-sided foundation that supports you, and it has both strong and not-so-strong sides. Your strengths are sides of the foundation that can stand strong on their own. Your weaknesses are sides of the founda-tion that are prone to developing cracks and holes. You don't necessarily need to replace the weak sides with strong ones, you just need to reinforce or repair those sections as needed. Prop them up with some additional structure. Patch the holes; reconnect the seams. For instance, even though managing is not a strength of mine, I'm not completely incapable of managing. I'm just not great at it. It's still an ability, although a weak one. It's a side of my foundation that is constantly crumbling, so I need to take measures to make sure it doesn't com-pletely collapse.

I once heard it put this way: *we need to improve our weaknesses only to the point where they don't make noise any more, that's it.* And improvement can come from building and improving our own skill set or finding outside resources. We can hire, delegate, design a process, or introduce automation to help compen-sate for our weaknesses.

I've done all the above to help me manage more effectively. I've hired people to run the ongoing parts of my business. I've handed off management responsibility to employees once I got a project started. I've created checklists to ensure we follow a process. I've employed new software that helps me automate certain types of activities. I still struggle because sometimes I remain hands-on a little too long. If I really want to play to my strengths and minimize my weaknesses, though, I need to hire, delegate, and automate much sooner. When I think about how many new and exciting projects I could start by doing this, I get totally energized and inspired.

Maybe you're great at marketing, but not great at selling/closing deals. You could partner up with someone who's much more of a closer.

If you excel at information gathering, but not so much at organizing the information once you have it, new software programs and apps are being developed every day to take that burden off your plate.

If your strength is delegating, but you're not so hot at following up or holding people accountable, you might consider hiring an assistant (or a virtual assistant) who can at least hold YOU accountable for following up with the people you need to.

HOW TO KNOW WHETHER A WEAKNESS IS CAUSING NOISE IN YOUR LIFE

It's pretty easy to figure out whether you have a weakness that needs fixed, improved, or minimized. Here are several red flags to look for:

- Your boss or coworkers complain about it (or worse, you get reprimanded for it). Most people allow a mistake or two, but hearing complaints from others might indicate that your weakness has become a regular, unwelcome occurrence.
- Your spouse, kids, or friends complain about it. Even if you don't hear about it at work, if the people closest to you point it out, you may have an issue that affects all areas of your life.
- People joke about it. While not as serious (maybe) as an actual complaint, sometimes people make jokes as a passive-aggressive way of pointing out something that bothers them.
- It slows down your progress or affects the quality of your work. This isn't always obvious to you, because you're in the middle of it. Asking for feedback

or comparing your progress against a "norm" of some type could help you identify potential areas of improvement.

- It bothers YOU. If something frustrates or irritates you, it's affecting the quality of your work or life, and it's worth paying closer attention to.

Again, don't feel like you have to completely fix every weakness in your life. There are many, many things we are not great at doing, and that's just fine. I can't hit a baseball. So what? My drawing skill is limited to stick figures (and even those are pretty bad). These weaknesses don't slow me down. I rarely need to do either of these things, nor does sucking at them negatively affect my work or my life in any way.

It does pay, however, to take a close look at what you consider weaknesses and decide whether they matter or not. Then minimize the ones you need to, and stop worrying about the rest.

Kryptonite, however, is a whole different story, and something you absolutely need to learn how to deal with.

AVOID YOUR KRYPTONITE

I can't think of a better metaphor that represents the external obstacles that keep us from maximizing our Ordinary Superpowers than Superman's Kryptonite.

In the story of Superman, there was only one thing that could bring the Man of Steel to his knees: Kryptonite, a mineral from his home planet of Krypton. Whenever he came in contact with it, he was stripped of his superhuman powers, which was devastating for Superman and even worse for humankind.

Kryptonite is not an internal weakness for Superman, it's an external force that diminishes his ability to use his superpowers.

It's an *obstacle*. And a pretty nasty one, too.

Superman can't just use more power and muscle past Kryptonite. He can't ignore it and pretend it's not there. He has to figure out how to remove it, remove himself from it, or navigate around it at a safe distance. He HAS to deal with it in order to continue using his powers at full strength.

SO, WHAT'S YOUR KRYPTONITE?

We all have external obstacles that keep us from doing our best work, or spending time the way we want to, or focusing on what we know will have the biggest impact. Do you know what your obstacles are?

Lack of Time Is Not the Problem (Not Really)

Many people will say lack of time is their biggest obstacle. While it can certainly *feel* that way, lack of time is never the problem. Lack of time is a *symptom*. What causes the lack of time is probably the Kryptonite. See if any of these ring a bell:

- You can't say no to requests from others (including friends, family, school, church, volunteer organizations, and your job).
- You focus on a million easy — but not particularly impactful — tasks.
- You focus only on "urgent" tasks (regardless of importance).
- You socialize a little too much.
- You socialmedialize (I just made that word up) a little too much.
- You spend a crazy amount of time managing all the "stuff" in your life.

There are more examples I could use, but you get the point. We often blame lack of time, but it's our lack of time management or poor ability to prioritize that is often the obstacle. We all have the same amount of time, and many people (with more on their plates than you have) manage their time extremely well. For those who don't, that's a weakness (an internal obstacle) like I described in the previous chapter. It's not Kryptonite (an external obstacle).

People ARE Often the Problem

Almost everyone has at least one person in their life who is complete Kryptonite to them. That person has the ability to completely distract you, upset you, interrupt you, control you, or otherwise keep you from using your Ordinary Superpowers as much as you could if he/she wasn't always getting in your way.

Sometimes the answer is to simply navigate away from that person, intentionally avoid them, or even break up with them.

But what if your Kryptonite is a co-worker, boss, or family member? You don't always have the power to remove those people completely from your life. But you may have the power to limit your exposure to them. It might be inconvenient for you, and it might feel completely unfair that YOU have to avoid THEM.

MANY PEOPLE WILL SAY LACK OF TIME IS THEIR BIGGEST OBSTACLE. WHILE IT CAN CERTAINLY FEEL THAT WAY, LACK OF TIME IS NEVER THE PROBLEM. LACK OF TIME IS A *SYMPTOM*.

To this I say, *"Suck it up, buttercup."* You can play the victim, or you can figure out how to keep rockin' your best self in spite of that Kryptonite disguised as a person.

IDENTIFY YOUR KRYPTONITE

Kryptonite can take many forms, personalized and individualized for each and every one of us. My Kryptonite likely doesn't affect you the same way it affects me, and vice versa.

Pay attention to what keeps you from spending quality time with your Ordinary Superpowers. One quick way to know what your Kryptonite may be is to observe what you *blame* for not using your powers more often. Maybe it's one of those time-management issues I mentioned earlier, or a person who sucks up too much of your energy. Kryptonite doesn't have to be something you dislike, just something that keeps you from using your powers to their fullest.

You might laugh at this, but as I'm writing this, two pieces of Kryptonite are my DOGS. I love my dogs; I would die for my dogs. But they have an amazing ability to completely destroy my focus. For instance, right now I'm trying hard to focus on writing, and yet every 15 minutes, they're begging me to let them out. Then two minutes later, they're barking to be let back in. When this happens, my superpower of communicating ideas through writing and speaking is completely obliterated. It took me 40 minutes just to write this paragraph.

So pretty soon, I'll do what I always do: I'll pack up my stuff and head to Starbucks. I'll navigate away from the Kryptonite. After a short period of refocusing (with no dogs barking), my superpower will restored, and I can get back to doing what I do best.

Here's the thing: I KNOW my dogs are going to distract me EVERY TIME I try to write at home, so you'd think I'd remember this and go straight to the coffee shop. But sometimes I forget (or I'm too lazy to put on pants), and I decide to give it another try at the dining room table. Of course, my two fur balls of Kryptonite never fail to do what they do best, and every time, my superpower is weakened until I navigate away from them. Someday I'll learn.

It's important to note that you don't have to navigate around your Kryptonite all the time, just when you want or need to use your Ordinary Superpowers (e.g., I will play with my dogs all day long — except when I'm trying to write). Of course, you may navigate away from a particular form of Kryptonite and realize you're better off without it in your life at all. That's your call, and you are 100% allowed to make it.

The world needs your Ordinary Superpowers at full strength, so I'm glad you're exploring everything you can do to protect against the forces that weaken them. Consistently using your powers at full strength also sets you up to experience the absolute highest level of impact and contribution that can only happen when you learn how to work with others to *multiply* your Ordinary Superpowers. Which means it's time to take the final step in our journey together.

READY TO ENHANCE?
Download the companion workbook at
www.markhenson.me/superpowerextras

STEP

4

MULTIPLY

"YOUR VISION WILL BECOME CLEAR ONLY WHEN YOU CAN LOOK INTO YOUR OWN HEART. WHO LOOKS OUTSIDE, DREAMS; WHO LOOKS INSIDE, AWAKES."

Carl Jung
(Psychiatrist Superhero)

CHAPTER 13

YOUR INVITATION TO RARE AIR

I know that if you put this book down right now and apply only what we've talked about so far, you'll find tons of value in it and life will improve for you and the people around you.

However, as I move through my own life, it remains painfully obvious that most people never do even the small amount of work it takes to identify their Ordinary Superpowers. Fewer people ever fully activate those powers. Still fewer make the effort to enhance them. And then there is the unusual breed that recognizes that it is possible to go much further than that.

That's where you are if you're on this page.

There's a great metaphor that describes where you'll be operating if you decide to fully maximize your Ordinary Superpowers. It's called *rare air*. When I hear that phrase, I always picture the elite climbers who reach the top of Mt. Everest. It takes effort that most aren't willing to make. But, oh, the accomplishment! And the view! Not many people get to see it. Not many get to breathe that air.

Work and commitment are not the only things required to reach rare air. Nobody climbs Everest alone; it takes an entire network of supporters. It also requires a few other elite climbers who are willing and able to go with you to the top.

In other words, as amazing as your Ordinary Superpowers may be, the "magic bullet" that will exponentially multiply your power, contribution, and impact is the realization you can't do it alone.

ENVISION MAXIMUM POWER

What would it look like if your Ordinary Superpowers could reach maximum power? What could you accomplish? How many people could you help? What amazing contributions could you make?

If you're like most people, you currently have no idea what maximum power looks like for you. Don't worry, I'm about to give you a glimpse into a whole new universe. My intent with the rest of this book is to push you beyond your comfort zone. Moving out of my comfort zone — even *imagining* having to move out of my comfort zone — makes my palms sweat, my heart skip a beat or two, and my adrenaline flow like it's coming from a fire hose. However, when I feel that way, I know that I'm being pushed/pulled/prompted/tempted/encouraged to grow.

I'll be honest, I'm not sure you'll ever completely know what your maximum power looks like. That's because the more you Activate, Enhance, and Multiply your powers, the more you will create capabilities and possibilities that don't currently exist. The boundaries of your powers will continue to expand as long as you continue to push those boundaries.

Three weeks after our first child was born, my wife and I had reached our maximum ability to function (or so I thought). I was so tired and overwhelmed, I could barely stand up. I wondered how in the world any couple would make the decision to have more than one child. At that moment, I truly didn't believe having a second child was possible — physically, mentally, or emotionally. So, of course, we had our second child just 18 months later. The amazing thing is that we had the second one by choice, not by accident (the first was also by choice, just to clarify). What changed between week 3 and week 32 (you know, when we, um, started the process of child #2)?

Somewhere along the way, we got better, stronger, and faster as parents. We figured out how to get enough sleep so we wouldn't crash our cars. We learned that we were actually able to keep another human being alive after all. And every day, it became more fun and rewarding.

NOBODY CLIMBS EVEREST ALONE.

We know now that we could have ten kids. Make no mistake, we are NOT having ten kids (right, honey?), but we know we could totally handle it. Having your first kid pushes the boundaries of your parental powers. Then you get used to it, and it becomes your new norm. Pretty soon you're saying crazy things like, "Let's have another baby."

We take massive steps in our lives — going to college, getting married, having babies, buying houses, and starting businesses — by first envisioning what life will be like when we get there. We spend a great deal of time painting the mental picture of a successful outcome. We picture our career taking an upward path, transforming our house into a magazine-worthy abode, raising our kids to be happy, healthy neurosurgeons, and starting a business that gives us purpose for the rest of our lives.

At the beginning, it is irrelevant whether any of it actually happens. What matters is that we envision it vividly enough to spark the all-important first step toward what's possible.

THINK SIGNIFICANTLY BIGGER

It would be way too easy to envision what "a little bit more" looks like. That comes to us naturally. We're wired to get up every day and do a little bit better than the day before. It's a much more challenging exercise to envision what a significantly bigger future looks like, but it can also be incredibly motivating and rewarding.

I am intentionally using a form of the word *significant* here. The meaning I intend is twofold. It means *noticeable, vast, or remarkable* — as in a *noticeably, vastly, or remarkably* bigger future. It also means *important*. I don't want you just to think about a bigger future, I want you to think about a better one. One where you spend your time on what's important — creating even more positive change in your life, the lives of others, and the world around you.

Revisit your Ordinary Superpowers. Think about what they look like right now in just one area of your life. What are you capable of at this moment if you use your powers at their current full strength? Who can you help? How much can you help them? What does your contribution look like? How much do you enjoy that part of your life?

As great as all of that may seem, now take it up ten notches. What if you could have significantly more impact than you're having right now? *What would help-ing twice as many or even ten times as many people look like? What if you could help even a single person a hundred times more than you're helping them now?* Imagine what a vastly greater amount of enjoyment, fulfillment, and prosperity would feel like!

As I'm writing this book, I reach around 5,000–10,000 people each week with my blog, email blasts, and social media posts. Ten times that is 50,000–100,000 people — a week! I know people who reach a million people (or more) each week, so theoretically I know it's possible. Emotionally, though, it scares me a little to know that I might affect that many people in a single week. It makes me take a closer look at what I'm putting out to the world, and question whether the quality is good enough. It yanks me pretty substantially out of my comfort zone.

Thinking significantly bigger isn't necessarily about the number of people you reach or help. For example, if one of your Ordinary Superpowers is generosity (sharing your money) and right now you're helping one person, cause, or organi-zation, what would it look like to give significantly more money to that person, cause, or organization? What would it look like to be able to give more money to more people, causes, and organizations? What would it look like to double that? What if you could multiply it 10 times? Now you're cookin'!

If you give generously of your time, what would it look like to give 20 percent of your time to a cause? Now imagine donating *half* of your time. What would happen then?

If your power is asking great questions, is there a time, place, or platform where your ability could have significantly more impact than it does now?

If you have the ability to entertain people with music, or comedy, or ventrilo-quism (yes, people still do that), what is the largest venue you've performed in so far? If you've only performed in your church or at a local bar, what would it look and feel like to perform at your city's largest theater, sports arena, or (dare I say it?) the Superbowl?

If your Ordinary Superpower is starting businesses, what would the world look like if you started ten businesses in the next ten years? Or if your next business was a hundred times bigger than the last one? What if the business you run right now grew a thousand percent in the next five years?

The first step toward a significantly bigger future is imagining it. The next step is believing you can create it.

I don't know about you, but I'm getting goosebumps.

Don't let your current circumstances limit your future possibilities. Just because something isn't possible *at this very moment* does not mean it's not possible. When you learn how to multiply your Ordinary Superpowers, bigger and better results can happen much faster than you think.

WHAT'S MISSING?

When you look at the future through a larger lens, you see an expanded, upgraded future. But you also see what's missing: all the abilities, talents, and skills that you lack to make that future a reality.

This is the moment when the seed of real multiplication is planted.

Because, perhaps for the first time, you realize you can't do it alone. You can't simply enhance your own superpowers enough to create the significantly bigger possibility you now see. Okay, maybe you can if you've got 80 more years on this planet. But, if you've read this far in the book, you'd probably like to manifest that bigger future long before you die. You know, so you've got a little time to enjoy it.

By the way, achieving a significantly bigger future is not the end. In fact, it may well be just the beginning. You might significantly increase your impact and contribution multiple times (and many people do!). Remember, as you Enhance and Multiply your Ordinary Superpowers, you are multiplying your *capabilities*. That means you're also multiplying your *possibilities*.

When you recognize you can't do it alone, then it's time to find your Superfriends.

CHAPTER 14

FIND YOUR SUPERFRIENDS

We've agreed you can't multiply your Ordinary Superpowers all by yourself. That means you'll need help — maybe lots of help. You'll need people around you who make your powers even more powerful and who complement your abilities with their own Ordinary Superpowers (ones that you don't have). I call those people Superfriends. Over the next few pages or so, you'll discover why they are so important and how to find your own.

THE DIFFERENCE BETWEEN THE PLAYGROUND AND THE PROS

On playgrounds across America, there are kids who are naturally talented at basketball. In fact, it would be hard to find an NBA or WNBA player who didn't start their journey on a hoop at a playground, in a driveway, or on the side of a barn somewhere.

These kids excel on the playground because of their natural abilities. The ones who desire to advance will eventually try out for a middle-school or high-school team. With good coaching, they'll learn how to activate and enhance their skills.

In some cases, and some places, a superstar can walk onto a mediocre team and carry them to victory after victory, perhaps even a championship. Those kinds of superstars have what I referred to at the beginning of the book as *extraordinary superpowers* — they're naturally gifted far beyond the rest of us. Superstars can typically carry a team only in middle school and maybe high school. After that, the field narrows, and the competition skyrockets. College teams employ full-time recruiters to attract the "best of the best" to their schools. The biggest and most prestigious college programs are filled with former high-school superstars, which makes it much harder for any one superstar to stand out. The NBA? Well, that's a collection of the best of the best of the best.

No matter how much of a superstar you are, to operate and contribute at a significantly higher level (like NBA championship level), you'll need a pretty super team to support you (and vice versa).

THE TEAM YOU PLAY WITH MATTERS

LeBron James — one of the true all-time superstars of basketball — didn't win an NBA championship until he surrounded himself with a better team (sorry, Cleveland fans, but it's true). He moved to Miami to play with a team that could support his desire and ability to win. Fortunately, Cleveland eventually strengthened their franchise, and he was able to return home and continue playing at a championship level, surrounded by other potential champions.

Steve Jobs was not solely responsible for the success of Apple, in spite of being portrayed as a lone-wolf maverick. He had the talents of Jony Ive and Tim Cook (and thousands of other top performers) on his team. He could not have created one of the most valuable companies in history without them.

Andy Stanley — who leads Northpoint Community Church in Atlanta (one of the largest churches in North America) — constantly praises the high quality of the people he's fortunate enough to have as direct reports and colleagues.

And of course, Iron Man could only achieve so much without the Avengers, and Batman didn't multiply his ability to fight evil until he partnered up with the Superfriends.

WHY SUPERFRIENDS ARE IMPORTANT

When I talk about your "team" from this point on, I'm referring to the people you work with, collaborate with, partner with, and who support you in what you're doing — especially when you're using your Ordinary Superpowers. Your team might be made up of friends, colleagues, mentors, family, and more.

TO MULTIPLY YOUR POWERS, YOU MUST HAVE PEOPLE IN YOUR CORNER WHO COMPLEMENT YOUR ABILITIES.

Any time you begin to operate at a higher level, you inevitably also rise above your current situation, and often your current team. To continue to operate at higher levels, you'll need a team that can support you at those levels.

I'm not saying you have to leave all your old friends behind, but there is some truth in the philosophy that you are the sum of the people you hang out with the most. As you examine your team, you may find you need help from some people who are not currently in your inner circle.

Since I started this chapter with a basketball theme, I'll stick with it. My daughter played in a community basketball league when she was in 7th and 8th grade. I had the privilege of being her coach. I can honestly say I taught her everything she knew about basketball in junior high. However, I can also honestly say that I taught her everything *I* knew as well. My basketball coaching ability was pretty much maxed out trying to herd 13-year-old girls into some semblance of a team. Needless to say, if she had wanted to play basketball in high school, she would have needed a coach who was capable of supporting her at that level. As much as I loved coaching her, my practical support at any higher level would have been limited to cheering her on from the stands.

To multiply your powers, you MUST have people in your corner who complement your abilities. That may be a new coach who can help you see a bigger picture, or new teammates who have superpowers that you don't have. It may be larger or higher-quality vendors or suppliers who can support what you're trying to achieve at the next level.

Have you ever watched *Shark Tank*? As I'm writing this, *Shark Tank* is a TV show where entrepreneurs and inventors pitch their product or company to potential investors. The #1 reason why they are on the show asking the investors for money isn't to get the money. It's to get the investor to play on their team, to be their coach, and to expand their connections — all things that are way more valuable than a pile of money. Money is relatively easy to get. Finding the right Superfriends is a bit more difficult, but so much more powerful than a pile of money in the long run.

One of my favorite examples of Superfriends is the partnership of Ron Howard and Brian Grazer. Together, they own Imagine Entertainment, and they have produced a mind-boggling string of blockbuster movies, TV shows, and digital content. Just a few of their more famous credits so far include *Cowboys & Aliens*, *The DaVinci Code*, *The Nutty Professor*, *Liar Liar*, *Arrested Development*, and *Friday Night Lights* (quite a range of genres and storylines, I might add).

They're both phenomenal storytellers, and they understand Hollywood from a lifetime of experience. But they both have unique abilities as well. Brian is a big-picture thinker who has a voracious appetite for learning and connection; Ron is a genius at making a story come alive and showcasing the best of what an actor can do. They realized early on that they multiply their powers by working together. Not only that, but they partner up with other amazing companies and talent as well. They understand that it takes a village of people using their superpowers to achieve amazing results. Their ability to be Superfriends to each other, and to find other Superfriends to play with, has empowered them to exponentially expand their powers over time. They have closets full of shiny trophies and bank accounts full of money to prove it.

WARNING: SOME FRIENDS MAY NOT BE SO SUPER

I'll be honest, I don't like this part of the journey. I'm not sure anyone does. However, there are some people on your current team who might not make the leap to a higher level with you. There are two reasons why:

1. *They might not be able to.*
   Life moves at a different pace for each of us. Circumstances can often keep people from taking another step right now. Kids, jobs, geography, and health are just a few of the parameters we all have to deal with, and sometimes those things keep us from moving on. Sometimes temporarily, sometimes longer.

2. *They might not want to.*
   People can be pretty stuck in their comfort zones. When you grow and expand, it can be a painful reminder to others that they are stuck where they are. Of course, they always have the power to grow and expand too, but it's not always easy. Look around; it's obvious many people don't want to do the work.

A few years ago, my coach at that time asked me a tough question. He asked, "When you reach the next level in your life, who will you surpass, who will you outgrow?"

I was shocked by the question. I had never thought about it; I'd assumed that I would just accumulate friends and colleagues throughout my entire life. I thought everyone would be along for the ride, to a certain degree. But as I considered my answer, I started to picture people that I knew wouldn't be on my team much longer, because they either wouldn't be able to keep up or wouldn't want to. It made me sad; I didn't want to let them go. Some of them were important to me at that time in my life.

For me, the toughest person to let go of was a close colleague of mine whom I spent a great deal of time with. We had supported each other for a long time. But I started to notice that every time I would share where I was headed, and how I was growing, she would say something slightly negative, or be passive-aggressive, or otherwise try to chip away at my plans and my optimism. I don't think she did it on purpose. It was just her natural reaction to the fact that I wanted to grow, and well, she didn't.

It's important to know that if you have to let someone go from your "team," you don't have to cut them completely out of your life. They're still good people, and you can still be friends. You just have to accept that they won't be in your corner the way they used to be. The colleague I mentioned above is still in my life, but to a much lesser degree. We still grab coffee and hang out a few times a year, but we're not collaborating and supporting each other like we once did. Like I said, it was tough to move on, but looking back on it now, it was a crucial step in my personal evolution. If I had kept that person in my inner circle, I'm pretty sure I wouldn't have taken a crack at some bigger opportunities that I have taken, including writing this book.

It took me a loooong time to realize I needed to surround myself with Superfriends. While I can be a social butterfly, I'm also a lone wolf in my professional pursuits. When it comes to building something, fixing something, or achieving anything, my first instinct is to attempt to do it all by myself. It took me years to realize that surrounding myself with an awesome team in my business was the key to growing it into what it has become. It's a lesson that I continue to learn in many other parts of my life as well. I'll probably always have lone-wolf tendencies, but now I see the power of seeking out Superfriends.

CHAPTER 15

A FEW MORE THINGS YOU MIGHT NEED

It would be fantastic if all it took to multiply your Ordinary Superpowers was finding a Superfriend or two. But unless your power is *easily finding all the Superfriends I need to achieve anything I want,* you'll likely need to gather a few more tools for your toolbox to multiply your powers and impact the world around you in a significant way.

Since everyone's Ordinary Superpower combination is unique to them, everyone also has a unique combination of "other stuff" they'll need to multiply their powers. There are no doubt some specific resources you will need, depending on what you're personally trying to achieve. That said, there are some needs that many of us have in common. Let's talk about those.

MONEY

Ah, yes, money. There's never enough, right? Actually, there are growing numbers of people who have learned how to live within their means and accomplish big things without a multimillion-dollar salary. That's exciting to me, because it shows that money is not the answer to all of our problems and desires.

That does not mean money doesn't matter. As you think about how you might multiply your Ordinary Superpowers, some of your efforts will undoubtedly take a few dollars out of your wallet. It's best to plan ahead for these expenses so you know how much money you'll need, where you might get it, and how long it will take to save it up or otherwise accumulate it.

Money for Projects

So, what will you need money for? Well, that depends on what you're trying to achieve. Almost any big dream or project requires more money than most people have in their savings account.

Money for Education

If you decide that multiplying your Ordinary Superpowers will require more education for you or someone else, that also carries a price tag. You might get by with a couple of books from Amazon or attending a conference or two, but some people will identify the need/opportunity to get a degree, finish a degree, or study a whole new area of interest. In general, the more education you need, the more money you'll need.

Money for Travel

Taking on bigger things often takes you further out of your neighborhood than you typically travel. Whether it's to work directly on a project, meet with your new Superfriends face-to-face, gather research, or gain education, you might need to spend some money on travel. Even a few extra tanks of gas can add up.

Money for Preparation

This has happened to me way more than once: I get excited about a new project and want to get started right away, so I start to purchase and gather the materials I'll need. It doesn't matter whether I'm purchasing a hammer or a special piece of software, it's easy to spend a pile of money before I even start working on the actual project itself. Starting any new venture usually requires investing some initial capital. That's not a bad thing. I'm just saying it helps to understand the cost before you start spending the cash.

On a personal note, when you do need money to take on bigger challenges and opportunities, I encourage you explore how to gather the money you'll need without taking on debt. I'm a big proponent of living a debt-free life. I believe it gives you much more freedom of choice and keeps your stress levels lower over the long haul. If the only way you can see to multiply your Ordinary Superpowers is to get a loan or to give away a big chunk of your company, I urge you to re-think your approach. Talk to some other people (the wiser the better) to see whether there might be another way.

RESOURCES

Money isn't the only resource you may need. Physical resources, like building supplies, are one form of resource. Expertise is another. Helping hands are yet another. While it's true that money can help you purchase resources, you might also find free resources just by looking around and asking others for help or guidance. When other people buy into your vision of what you're trying to achieve, they will often do whatever they can to assist. And sometimes they'll even commit vast resources to support your mission, at little or no cost to you.

KNOWLEDGE

When you decide to multiply your Ordinary Superpowers, one thing you will likely discover is that you're missing some knowledge that would help you multiply your powers to their greatest extent. This is different than simply enhancing your powers, which is more about incrementally improving your actual powers.

The knowledge I'm referring to here is the "other" knowledge you might need to take on a bigger project, challenge, or opportunity. For example, one of my powers is communicating ideas through writing. During the course of writing this book, I enhanced my writing powers by reading some books about how to write and communicate with style and clarity. However, to truly multiply my writing powers, I quickly realized I would need a team of people around me with a whole range of superpowers that I don't have, including editing, designing, printing, and promoting a book.

Yes, you can write and self-publish a book all by yourself. I've seen many examples of books published by one-man-bands. I have also noticed the quality of those books isn't what I wanted for mine, nor do they seem poised or prepared to appeal to a larger audience.

These are just some of the big things that many of us will need to consider as we multiply our Ordinary Superpowers. It's impossible to list all the things everyone may need, but I wanted to spark your brain here so that you think ahead a bit. Everyone has a unique combination of powers and will multiply them in unique (and countless) ways. As you entertain the idea of expanding your impact with your Ordinary Superpowers, I encourage you to take some time to think through the costs and needs that are beyond what is currently available to you, and create an idea of how you'll get them when the time comes. You'll definitely set yourself up for a faster and much less bumpy journey if you do.

READY TO MULTIPLY?
Download the companion workbook at
www.markhenson.me/superpowerextras

WITH GREAT POWER...

I have two questions for you as I wrap this book up:

1. *What CAN you do now with your Ordinary Superpowers?*
2. *What WILL you do now with your Ordinary Superpowers?*

By absorbing this book, you've embarked on a journey to Discover, Activate, Enhance, and Multiply your Ordinary Superpowers. Every step in the process gives you greater and greater power, and the chance to make a bigger and better difference in your life and the lives of the people you encounter from now on.

Through this process, you've clarified how you already use your powers, and hopefully you've identified many ways in which you can proactively use them moving forward.

But *can* and *will* are two very different things, aren't they?

You've no doubt heard the quote, *"With great power comes great responsibility."* It appeared in the August 1962 edition of the *Spider-Man* comic book and at least one of the more recent *Spider-Man* movies. It has also been attributed to Voltaire, Winston Churchill, and Teddy Roosevelt.

Self-discovery often leads to choices and opportunities you may not have ever considered before. Maybe it has revealed something specific. Perhaps you've opened up a thousand new possibilities to contribute to the world at a significantly higher level. Or maybe you've just discovered there is one person in your immediate circle you can help on a much deeper level, now that you know how to.

It is quite possible that you now have more possibilities than you know what to do with. Not a bad problem to have, but not necessarily an easy one, either. When you have many possibilities, it can be hard to decide which to pursue. So, how do you decide what to do from here?

You could make a list of pros and cons for each of your powers or possibilities. You could create a priority matrix to determine where to spend your time and energy to get the biggest bang for your buck. You could ask your coach or a trusted advisor to help you choose. Or...

You could simply do what lights you up the most. Which of your Ordinary Superpowers are the most fun for you to use?

Which activities that use your Ordinary Superpowers do you personally get the most satisfaction from?

There is absolutely nothing wrong with taking this approach, because we're talking about the talents and skills that have passed the test of an Ordinary Superpower: *They come naturally to you, you're better at them than most, they help the most people (or help people the most), and you enjoy using them.* They all help you contribute at your highest levels, they all help people, and they all light you up. So why not use the ones that light you up the most?

Once I discovered and clarified what my Ordinary Superpowers were, I faced this exact struggle. There were so many ways I could use my powers for good, and I became paralyzed by the sheer number of choices. So, I eventually decided that I would pursue the one that seemed the most fun for me at the time. That decision eventually led me to writing this book. Writing is one of the most satisfying activities that I do. Funny, it's also how I help people the most people (and help people the most).

I would not be surprised at all if you, too, found out the Ordinary Superpower you enjoy using the most is also how you'll do the most good in the world.

OF COURSE, THIS IS JUST THE BEGINNING

What I find most exciting about the concept of Ordinary Superpowers is that you can always Discover more about them. You can always find new ways to Activate them. There is never-ending knowledge to help you Enhance them. And your ability to Multiply them is limited only by your ability to find people who strengthen and complement your powers — and the last time I checked, there were 7.125 billion people on this planet (yes, I Googled it). I'm pretty sure a few of them would love to be your Superfriends.

Even during the course of writing this book, I have discovered more about my Ordinary Superpowers, and I've even discovered one that I didn't fully recognize before: *I include the unincluded.* I've realized that my radar always seems to start beeping when people are being left out of something, and I gently pull them into the conversation, space, or activity with a minimal amount of fuss.

That's what happens when you spend time with this concept and this material, you continue to learn more and more about yourself.

So, no matter where you are in your Ordinary Superpower journey, and no matter how much you may have already achieved, it is always the beginning. There is always more to learn about yourself, and always more to be done to make a positive difference on every level, from the smallest personal problems to the grandest worldwide challenges.

LET'S TAKE THIS JOURNEY TOGETHER

I invite you to continue learning, and to keep fully engaging with your Ordinary Superpowers. And I want to help you in any way I can. Here are a few ways that are already in place:

Visit My Website
www.markhenson.me is the home base for my work and the best source for ongoing information about Ordinary Superpowers. You'll find information about the book, my speaking, my blog, and more. It's also a great place to refer people you share the ideas in this book with.

Download the Workbook
If you did a quick first read of this book and you're now ready to dive into the various activities, visit www.markhenson.me/superpowerextras to download the free companion workbook.

Attend a Superpower Summit Workshop
The Superpower Summit is a full-day, fully immersive deep-dive into Ordinary Superpowers. It's like this book, but in real life, in real time. We host several Superpower Summits each year at my worldwide HQ, sparkspace, in Colum-

SELF-DISCOVERY OFTEN LEADS TO CHOICES AND OPPORTUNITIES YOU MAY NOT HAVE EVER CONSIDERED BEFORE.

bus, Ohio, and other locations around the world. Visit www.markhenson.me/ superpowersummit/ for upcoming events.

Connect with Me on Social Media
As of the writing of this book, I have several social media accounts, but I'm most active on Facebook and Instagram (find me on both as markbhenson). You know how fast social media moves, though, so look for me on whatever platform you currently use. There's a good chance I'll be there, too.

Email Me
I'm very responsive to email, at least until this book is a *New York Times* Best Seller and I get a million emails a day! Drop a note to mark@markhenson.me sometime and let me know what your Ordinary Superpowers are, how you're using them, and any questions you may have, or just say hi. I'd love to connect with you.

ONE FINAL THOUGHT: YOU DON'T HAVE TO CHANGE THE WORLD TO CHANGE YOUR WORLD

I've witnessed a growing theme in our culture. Countless books, blogs, workshops, speakers, etc., are preaching messages of:

"Be legendary."

"Do something epic with your life."

"Change the world."

The problem with these messages is that they put SO much pressure on us! Change the world? Be legendary? That's a pretty big challenge, don't you think? These messages have led so many down the wrong path — including me. They encourage us to chase fame. They encourage us to do everything we can to be perceived as awesome. They tell us that if we don't live an "epic" or "legendary" life, then we are missing out big time and not living the life we were meant to live.

I'm going counter-culture on this one:

Stop trying to be famous. Stop trying to make everything you work on, or participate in, seem epic or legendary.

Instead, just breathe. Take some time to explore what would feel truly significant to YOU. Let go of the lofty, legendary status that the world is pushing you to pursue. Status is not significance.

Let me repeat: STATUS IS NOT SIGNIFICANCE.

Instead of trying to "be legendary," why not just try to be you? Why not spend your time and energy using your unique set of talents and skills in ways that light you up, regardless of what anyone else thinks? Why not contribute to your job, business, family, and community in ways that truly make a difference, even if they don't make you trend on Twitter?

I don't know anyone who is truly epic or legendary who tried to be perceived that way. They simply live their most authentic self, doing stuff they love to do. When they do that, they end up contributing at their highest levels, helping the most people, and feeling incredibly fulfilled. They end up creating positive change in their lives, the lives of others, and the world around them.

And wouldn't you know it, the rest of the world sees that as pretty epic and legendary (which is not the reason to do it, but you get my point, right?).

So, yes, you might work on solving large-scale, worldwide problems, launch powerful new products, or build wildly successful ventures, and I hope some of you do. But what I sincerely want you to do from here is to listen to your Ordinary Superpowers. Let them lead you to contribute meaningfully to others every chance you get.

I can't wait to see what you and your Ordinary Superpowers will do.

INSTEAD OF TRYING TO "BE LEGENDARY," WHY NOT JUST TRY TO BE YOU?

ACKNOWLEDGMENTS

Since this is my first book, I feel like I need to thank everyone who has ever been a part of my life. So if you're one of those people, thank you. I truly believe that you helped shape who I am, how I think, and how this book turned out.

That said, I need to say thanks to some individuals, specifically:

Eve. I could write you a long, mushy love letter here, but since I just wrote one of those in a card for our 26th wedding anniversary, I'll just say you are, well, everything an entrepreneur/author/husband could want in a woman.

Ava and Marissa. You may never read the whole book, but I know you'll read this part. One of my favorite things in life is being your dad. Watching you grow up has inspired me more than you'll ever know. Out of all the people in the world who I hope discover their Ordinary Superpowers, it's you two.

Mom and Dad. I'll never, ever be able to express how grateful I am that I got you two when God was handing out parents. I knew you supported and loved me when I was still a kid, and somehow it feels like you've done even more for me now that I'm all grown up.

My current team at sparkspace: Jason, Leah, Holly, and Harris. I literally couldn't have written this book without you. You run sparkspace better than I ever did, and you've given me something that most authors would kill for: the time and freedom to get this project done.

My 100% Columbus-based book-creation team: Andrea Clute, Terry Rohrbach and the crew at FORT, and West-Camp Press. When I first had the idea to produce this book start-to-finish using entirely local resources, I never thought I'd find such truly world-class people and resources in my own backyard.

Jon Petz. I believe you may be my #1 cheerleader. Your encouragement, friendship, and coffee conversations are never taken for granted, believe me.

Jason Barger. Wisdom + humor is how I describe you in my head (and now on paper). That combo has been more helpful to me than you know. Thanks for sharing your advice, your process, and several rounds of Mexican food with me during this journey.

Kary Oberbrunner. To have such an accomplished author as a friend and fan is an incredible thing. I can't thank you enough for sharing my story and my work with the world.

Gina Pellegrini. Although I may have been incredibly slow to heed your advice sometimes, you have helped me create more margin in my life than I thought possible.

Erin Coughlin. Thanks for pushing me to take a sabbatical. Although it took over a year to sink in, there is no question in my mind I would have never started this book without taking that time off.

Mike Clouse. Thanks for using your superpower of coaching on me even before I hired you as a coach. Your encouragement, prayers, and friendship are priceless.

Finally, to everyone who has told me *"You should write a book,"* or *"I can't wait to read your book,"* or *"I love your blog,"* or *"Your weekly emails are the only ones I read,"* you have unknowingly pushed me to keep writing even when I have doubted myself. Especially when I have doubted myself. My wish — that I wish with every ounce of my being — is that you will love this book, because you deserve it. I hope it serves you well.